Citizen Soldier –

Carl T. Jones

Raymond B. Jones

Other books by Raymond B. Jones:

Southern Turkey Hunting – A Family Affair
The Farm in Jones Valley

Dedication

This book is dedicated to the memory of my father, Carl T. Jones, who was a true citizen-soldier and the patriarch of our family. My father, in his relatively short fifty-eight year life, was a tremendous influence on literally hundreds of people. In addition to being my hero, he was my father, friend, business partner and hunting buddy. Carl Jones projected a stabilizing influence on all of our family and our employees as well as his friends and associates. More than any other leader I have known, he was always way out front because he had that unusual talent of leadership that made people want to follow his direction.

My father came from a long line of pioneers, patriarchs and leaders that you will read about in this book. If somehow we could poll all those family members and associates who knew him, I think the vote would be unanimous that Carl T. Jones was a consummate example of an outstanding leader and citizen soldier.

Raymond B. Jones

Table of Contents

Acknowledgments v

Introduction vii

Part I 1

    Chapter 1 – The Big Spring 1

    Chapter 2 – Mountain Fork Creek 5

    Chapter 3 – The Pioneer Patriarch 11

    Chapter 4 – "The WAH" 17

    Chapter 5 – A New Beginning 31

    Chapter 6 – G. W. Jones 37

    Chapter 7 – The Family of Elvalena and G.W. Jones 43

Part II 55

    Chapter 8 - Gearing Up For War 55

    Chapter 9 - 151st Combat Engineer Battalion 61

    Chapter 10 - Attu 71

    Chapter 11 - Kiska 79

    Chapter 12 - More Alaskan Experiences of Carl Jones ... 89

    Chapter 13 - Change of Venue 99

    Chapter 14 - Warminster 105

    Chapter 15 - Normandy 113

    Chapter 16 - Belgium / Holland 125

    Chapter 17 - Germany 135

    Chapter 18 - Going Home 143

Part III 151

    Chapter 19 - Starting Over 151

    Chapter 20 - Kentucky 31 Fescue 159

    Chapter 21 – Huntsville's #1 Salesman 167

Chapter 22 – Mister Carl 173
Chapter 23 - The HIC Center 181
Chapter 24 - Exciting Times 189
Chapter 25 - The New Airport.. 197
Chapter 26 - The Loss.. 203
EPILOGUE 209

Table of Figures

Isaac and Joseph Criner at the Big Spring - 1804 4

Isaac Criner's Second House (Page 64 of Huntsville Historical Review) 8

Isaac Criner's Tombstone in Mt. Paran Cemetery, New Market, Alabama 15

The only known image of Milus E. "Bushwhacker" Johnston 28

Nathan Bedford Forrest 29

Major George Washington Jones' Coat on display at the Civil War Museum near Clanton, Alabama 36

G. W. Jones in His Office at 307 Franklin Street 42

The Jones boys at National Guard camp 45

Portrait of G.W. Jones 60

Admiral's Staff, Adak, Alaska (Carl Jones in Center), November 1943 69

Carl "Sourdough" Jones, Kodiak, Alaska, December 1941 70

Massacre Bay Beach 75

Engineer Bulldozer Stuck in Muskeg 76

Over 1,000 Japanese Bodies, Mostly by Suicide 77

How the Battle Was Fought 78

Kiska Plan Of Attack 84

Engineers and Others Used 678 Wide Track Tractors Moving Cargo Off the Beach 85

Japanese Tunnel, Kiska 86

5,500 Toboggan Sleds Were Used To Move Supplies Inland. Excellent Muskeg Transportation 87

The Bear Attack 97

Ed being decorated with the Legion of Merit medal, Nome, 1944 98

Mule Barn About 1945 104

Mule Barn Today 104

Boyton Manor in Warminster 110

Worth Fighting For 111

Copy of Communique From Eisenhower 112

Carl T. Jones 120

German Cavalry Saddle and Helmet 121
St. Lo 122
Seine River Crossing 123
Ottenhoff Family 133
Nelson's Grave 134
Siegfried Line 1944 141
The Author with Nazi Flag taken from Aachen, Germany in 1944 142
Margraten Cemetery 142
VJ Day Photo 150
Hereford Cattle Grazing In Jones Valley 1950 166
Thornton Research Park 172
Sheep grazing in Jones Valley, circa 1954 179
Carl T. Jones, "Mr. Huntsville", circa 1960 180
HSV Times newspaper announcing Explorer I satellite 186
Gathering at Court House Square, Jan 31, 1958 187
Cave Picture: Walter Jones holding a map / Ray Jones holding the rope ladder 193
Old Airport Terminal 195
Airport Cave Explosion/1967 202

Acknowledgments

Issac Criner ---- family patriarch, Madison County's first white settler and one who originally instilled many valuable traits into our family.

G. W. Jones ---- civil engineer, Alabama State Senator, 1927-1931, and the father of the subject of this book.

Elvalena M. Jones ---- granddaughter of Isaac Criner and the grandmother who told me Civil War and family stories for many years.

Carl T. Jones ---- my father, whose profound influence must be acknowledged.

Walter B. Jones ---- my uncle who also served as Alabama State Geologist for over 30 years as well as one of my mentors in life.

Elizabeth M. Jones ---- my wonderful partner and wife for almost 55 years. Her influence on my life and her encouragement to write this book cannot be measured.

Lisa J. Yokley ---- my daughter and primary editor who was a major influence on me to write, edit and publish this book, without which it would never have been printed.

Mark H. Yokley ---- my son-in-law who handled the technical aspects of assembling the book for publishing.

May J. Patterson ---- my daughter who added substantial layout and editing advice.

Judge Lynwood Smith ---- United States District Judge and friend who improved this book through a comprehensive editing.

Dr. William Gardner ---- one of my cousins who furnished family dates and confirmation.

George Jones ---- another cousin who furnished family dates and confirmation.

Dr. Douglas P. Jones and wife Bonnie ---- family historian and cousin whose research of family history, particularly of the Civil War, was a great help.

Kathleen P. Jones and Pauline J. Gandrud ---- aunts of mine who prepared a family genealogy all the way back in time to the year 1628 which was also a great help.

Howard Sanderford ---- State of Alabama Representative who assisted in verification of dates of service.

Nancy Dupree ---- State of Alabama Archivist who also researched dates of service.

Introduction

This book is primarily about the life of Carl T. Jones, with a special emphasis on his World War II experience.

The Carl T. Jones family story really began in 1804 with the coming of his great grandfather, Isaac Criner, to North Alabama. Isaac Criner was the first white settler to live in what is now Madison County, Alabama and he remained near the town of New Market for the rest of his life.

From this early beginning, Part I of this book follows the lineage of Isaac Criner for three generations which encompasses the Civil War, World War I, World War II and the farming and other enterprises attempted by his extended family. The early family stories from the 19th century were conveyed to me by my grandmother, Elvalena M. Jones, as I sat at her knee as a young man.

Part II of this book contains World War II information gleaned primarily from the journals of my father as he fought through the war in Alaska and northern Europe. Being a civil engineer, Carl was very detailed and left meticulous records, complete with photographs, as the war progressed.

Part III is composed of efforts by Carl and his family as they sought to rebuild their lives after World War II. Carl and his brother Edwin worked diligently to expand the civil engineering business that was started by their father, G. W. Jones in 1886. Additionally, a 2,500 acre farm just south of Huntsville, Alabama was developed into a cattle operation by the brothers and is thought today to be one of the largest working urban farms in America. This book concludes with the death of Carl T. Jones in 1967.

It has been a labor of love for me to research the lives of my ancestors. I wish I had the penmanship to more adequately and vividly describe their lives. Suffice it to say that I am most humbled to be counted in the lineage of Isaac Criner, G. W. Jones and my father Carl T. Jones.

Raymond B. Jones
2015

Part I

Chapter 1 – The Big Spring

Following a well-used Indian trail, two horses and two pack mules steadily moved southwest along the trail carrying two men and their equipment. The trip was to last three weeks, so considerable food and woodworking gear was being transported. It was the Fall of 1804. Their reason for the trip was to locate a big spring that Indian lore had mentioned for years. It was located about 10 miles north of the Tennessee River near the termination of the Indian trail. Supposedly, this spring never went dry and its water flow was more significant than any other spring in the area. In addition, there was plenty of timber for a cabin and the soil was exceedingly rich.

The men's names were Isaac Criner and his uncle, Joseph Criner. They both had a strong desire to find better farmland and to build cabins and move their families from Lincoln County, Tennessee to what is now North Alabama. They camped along the way and forded a small river and several creeks which were present in the area. The Indian name "Alabama" means "land of many rivers", of which North Alabama certainly has its share. Since the time of this trip was in the Fall, the stream crossings were easier than they would have been in the Winter or Spring.

Somewhere just east of what is now Chapman Mountain, and west of the Flint River crossing, they pitched their last camp en route to the spring. It was a nice place to camp with plenty of grass for the horses and mules and there was an abundance of firewood. Sometime during the night, they were awakened by screams coming from the timbered area surrounding the land. They retrieved their guns and waited while they listened to the intermittent screams throughout the night. Even though they were following an Indian trail (later named Winchester Road), they had not seen any Indians along the way. Still, the screams persisted for hours.

  As daylight approached, one of the men saw a cougar running in the woods and concluded that they had been kept awake all night by mountain lion screams. They broke camp early and began the climb over Chapman Mountain. The spring in question lay only about three miles from the southwestern base of the mountain and was easy to find. Several Indian trails led to this big spring, highlighting the fact that water is usually the direct basis for the spread of civilization. Indian campsites were numerous, yet they saw no Indians until they reached the spring. Upon arriving at the spring, they found several Indian women washing garments and several Indian men mounted on horseback in the wooded area above the spring.

  These Indians were Cherokee and were a peace loving people. The Cherokee Indians were very advanced as a nation, a people with walled cities, an alphabet, and a system of government. They were planters as well as hunters and were generally friendly to the white man. Even though the Criner men felt comfortable around the Indians, they positioned their tent adjacent to a high bluff overlooking the spring. Hand tools and other items of metal were brought into the tent at night. The Cherokee didn't seem to be a dangerous threat to these strangers, but they would readily take anything of value if left unattended. Now that the legendary spring had been found and a temporary camp established, they began to explore the area for a permanent cabin site and to cut and notch as many logs as practical. The Criners decided to call the spring "The Big Spring", a name that has remained to this day.

   The area above the spring offered the most desirable location for a cabin site as it was well drained with plenty of building logs nearby. The downstream area to the west was swampy as it attempted to absorb the tremendous flow of water from the spring. (Later, in the 1950s, a hydrologist calculated the Big Spring flow at 24 million gallons per day). The weather was hot and the men were constantly fighting mosquitoes, rattlesnakes, and had even seen a few black bears near the spring. Undaunted, they worked tirelessly cutting and notching logs for the cabins they hoped to build the following Spring. These logs were carefully stacked up off the ground to prevent them from deteriorating until they returned with their families.

   When they had assembled enough logs to construct at least two buildings, they loaded their horses and mules for the trip back to Lincoln County, Tennessee. The route for the return trip was the same, except they chose not to camp in the mountain lion area. The Flint River and the numerous small streams obstructing the trail seemed to be crossed easier than on the initial trip.

They admired the Mountain Fork Creek area around what is now New Market, Alabama as an alternative site to the Big Spring area. Satisfied with their expedition, they were glad to finally make it back home. The Winter and early Spring would be used to prepare for the return trip to the Big Spring to build from the prepared cabin logs. Hopefully, the Spring season of 1805 would be dry, making the stream crossings easier and the trail footing firmer. The two Criner families endured their last Winter in Tennessee with the anticipation of their new homes in the rich and fertile land of what is now Madison County, Alabama.

Isaac and Joseph Criner at the Big Spring - 1804

Chapter 2 – Mountain Fork Creek

In April of 1805, the Criner caravan started south. It consisted of the two families, Isaac's and Joseph's, their horses, mules, wagons, milk cow, chickens and dogs. The Spring of 1805 was wet, and progress was slow at best. The travel time was about half the pace that it took Joseph and Isaac the previous Fall. They had some mechanical trouble with one of the wagons near what is now Elora, Tennessee, which cost them several days delay. Back on the wet trail and with more rain, they decided to make camp and rest the group when they reached Mountain Fork Creek. There was a good campsite near a bluff that overlooked the creek as well as the area where the town of New Market is today. (This campsite was later named the Mt. Paran Campground and Cemetery.)

During this rest stop, the men explored the area primarily upstream along the creek. They were quick to notice the fine timber and grassland as they explored to the east. Some of the best agricultural land they had seen lay in the small valleys from which creeks flowed. They were particularly impressed with one rather high hill that jutted above the confluence of two valleys where the creeks combined to make up Mountain Fork Creek. The entire area offered everything the families were looking for in a house site. That night they had a family meeting in which they discussed the newly discovered area as an alternative home site. Most probably the discussion also included the mosquitoes, bears, and the abundance of Indians at the Big Spring. In any event, this upstream bluff site was chosen and would become their new home.

It didn't take long for the Criners to cut and notch logs for the new cabins, as well as to prepare a garden spot and build corrals for the livestock. Fish from the creek were plentiful, and wild game abounded in the area. They also noticed a succulent plant growing in the tail waters of the creek and in the nearby springs. The plant was watercress, and it was growing in abundance. Watercress is very tasty and makes an excellent salad. Years later, a watercress company would cultivate and grow watercress in abundance on these same lands and offer it for sale all over the eastern United States. The company was named The Dennis Watercress Company, and they promoted Huntsville as being "The Watercress Capitol of the World".

The Criner families settled into their new home place, which would serve Isaac well for most of the next 75 years. Not long after this new homestead was established, the Criners had a visit from a man named John Hunt and his traveling companion, Andrew Bean. Strangely enough, they were traveling along the same Indian trail in search of the Big Spring. Isaac and Joseph told their story of traveling to the spring the previous year. They also told Hunt about the logs they had cut and notched at the spring and offered the logs to Hunt if he decided to build a cabin there.

Hunt and Bean spent the night with the Criners and traveled on toward the Big Spring the next day. Several weeks later Bean stopped back by on his way to Salem, Tennessee and told them that Hunt had decided to settle at the Big Spring, but that he was going home. History records John Hunt as being the first white settler to permanently live at the Big Spring. Hunt was quickly followed by several settlers, all seeking fortune and a new life. The settlement was first called Hunt's Spring, then Twickenham, and finally Huntsville, reflecting the name of its first settler.

The Mississippi Territory was organized in 1798, and North Alabama was included in 1804. The next year, Isaac and Joseph Criner and their families came to live in what is now Madison County. Patented land was available to settlers at a very reasonable price (about $2 per acre), causing a large migration to North Alabama after 1804. By 1808, a census listed 353 families and 2,223 residents, including slaves, inhabiting Madison County. There were at least three areas in the county that were the most popular to these early settlers, namely Hunt's Spring, Three Forks of Flint, and the Market area (the town was later named New Market).

Following the lead of Isaac and Joseph Criner, several other families by the names of Davis, Moore, Smith, Whitman, Miller, Bayless, Jones, Bragg, and McBroom also came to settle in Madison County. These were hardy, adventuresome people, both men and women. They came to farm this productive and beautiful land, seeking for themselves a new life as pioneers into what is now Madison County, Alabama.

Isaac Criner would continue to live on that same bluff home site until his death in 1876. In 1814, Isaac married Nancy McCain and they had eleven children, eight girls and three boys. Isaac and his family survived the Civil War in this location and farmed and made a home there for over 70 years. Sometime after building the original cabin, Isaac built a more substantial two-story house with two chimneys and a large front porch.

Isaac Criner's Second House (Page 64 of Huntsville Historical Review)

Joseph Criner lived at the original bluff site alongside Isaac's family for several years, but eventually built a home east of Gurley near Harrison's Cove. Like Isaac, Joseph farmed for a living, raised a family, and was one of Madison County's first settlers.

Little did Isaac realize the future influence his offspring would have on Madison County, Alabama, and the Nation. This humble beginning on Mountain Fork Creek would eventually produce civil engineers, architects, physicists, farmers, land surveyors, geologists, , Ph.Ds, M.D.'s, nurses, and several businessmen. The family also included State of Alabama Senators, several veterans serving in the Civil War, World Wars I and II, as well as numerous civic leaders.

Someone once said that, "Anyone can count the seeds in an apple, but only God can count the apples in a seed." Pioneer Isaac Criner obviously sowed the right kind of seed that has and will influence Alabama and the Nation for generations to come. Like any pioneer who blazes a trail to new lands, Isaac must have had that domineering spirit that it takes to complete the task. He sought a place for a new home and farm, raised a big family, and passed that independent spirit on to subsequent generations. All Americans have been blessed by pioneers from the beginning of our country and somewhere on the list, North Alabama has also been blessed by men like the pioneer named Isaac Criner.

Chapter 3 – The Pioneer Patriarch

Life for the Isaac Criner family, like most of the early pioneers, was a struggle at best. Every scrap of time was used to survive and build. Growing food consumed most of the effort. In addition to growing a vegetable garden, there was equal emphasis on raising livestock such as pigs, cattle, poultry, horses, and mules. Most likely, the draft horses and mules received the most care, for without them transportation and plowing of the fields could not be accomplished.

Nearby fields were turned each Spring or Fall for the planting of field crops such as corn, sorghum, peas, and later on, cotton. The soil was very fertile, since it was virgin soil that had never been cultivated. Commercial fertilizer had not been developed in the early 1800s, so the only nourishment for the garden or the fields was animal waste. The Indians also taught them to save fish parts when cleaning the fish caught from Mountain Fork Creek for use as a fertilizer.

Hunting and trapping in the Winter helped supply the family with meat to eat and animal hides for clothing, as well as fertilizer for the crops. Hogs were very important as a meat source for the family. They began to fatten the hogs sometime in late Summer when the corn crops began to ripen. Cobs, shucks, grain, and anything else the hogs would eat, was fed to fatten them in anticipation of slaughter coinciding with the frost in early October. Everything about the hog was used – the fat made lard and soap, the muscle cuts (hams and shoulders) were salt cured and smoked, the hooves were used for buttons, and various scraps of meat from other cuts were ground into sausage. "Hog killing day," when the first cold snap arrived, was a big affair and it took the whole family to process the meat.

Seed for planting was also a very important item for the family. Implements for tilling the soil, such as plows, rakes, hoes, chains, etc., were treasured. Nothing was wasted, unlike in our society today. We live in a virtual "throw away" era; when something breaks, we simply go buy another. In Isaac's day, if something broke they fixed it. One thing that most early pioneer families would not be without was an anvil. With an anvil, most any piece of metal could be heated and beaten into shape or repaired for future use. Clothing, as well as shoes, were repaired and worn for years, or in the children's case, "handed down". Fashion, at least in the early days, was not a consideration, because survival and protection from the elements was most important.

Isaac Criner was evidently a man who could handle virtually any situation. As time passed, he expanded his fields and livestock holdings to become a very successful man for his day. He traded vegetables, grain, cotton, animal hides, and livestock with the Indians and settlers that came to the area. He was very resourceful in building his family farm and living compound.

Sometime in the 1830-40 time-frame, Isaac added several slave families to his farm on Mountain Fork Creek. Isaac and Nancy McCain had married in 1814 and now had eleven children, so the demand for labor to produce more food and fiber had increased. These new black families melded into the family farm, working side by side, laboring for the purpose of providing food, clothing and shelter for the assembled colony. These new families were hard workers and brought some needed talent to Isaac's farm. Over the years, these families grew close to the Isaac Criner family and the combined group forged ahead and prospered. If history had to choose just one phrase that described these hardy early American pioneers it would be this: "they persevered and endured many hardships to make a better life and home for their families".

One of Isaac's children, Martha Woodson Criner, was born in 1836. She would go on to have a profound effect on the future lineage of Isaac. This young girl grew up on the Mountain Fork Creek farm. She fell in love with a young man named William Henderson Moore who lived in Lincoln County, Tennessee. By the time their courtship was in full bloom in the late 1850s, war talk was in the air, and the Civil War seemed to be inevitable. Early on, William was involved with an army unit, the 1st Tennessee Regiment, which was already training for duty. With the uncertainty of the future, William and Martha decided to put marriage on hold until the issue of northern oppression was settled.

Isaac would not actually fight in the war, but it would exact a heavy toll on his family and farm compound. He was resourceful enough to organize a family defense system of the buildings, livestock, grounds, and particularly their food sources. Every member of the little colony under Isaac's defense plan would have a duty to perform, when and if the Yankees would raid the compound. These duties were practiced repeatedly and all, bond and free, prayed that war would never come, but such would not be the case.

Isaac would survive the Civil War, passing away in 1876 at the age of 93. One trait that family stories perpetuated about Isaac was that every morning he would descend the bluff from his house to Mountain Fork Creek, and he would proceed to wash his beard and head. Sometimes in the Winter when he returned home his beard would be frozen. Nevertheless, he reportedly never varied from that practice.

Isaac Criner, Madison County's first white settler, was laid to rest four months before his 94th birthday in Mt. Paran Cemetery near the place where he and his uncle Joseph had camped in 1804. He never wavered in his love for the Mountain Fork Creek area, and in promoting a better life for his family. According to my grandmother, Isaac lived a clean life, avoiding harmful personal habits, and encouraging his children to do the same. Either from necessity or guidance, he taught his children to work, a trait that mostly carries on in his extended family today. Thus from this hardy, adventuresome pioneer patriarch, a long lineage of family would evolve that would have a profound influence on the County, State, and Nation in the years to come.

Isaac Criner's Tombstone in Mt. Paran Cemetery, New Market, Alabama

References for this chapter: Huntsville Historical Review, 2008 and conversations with my grandmother

Chapter 4 – "The WAH"

The "War Between the States" has been called, depending upon the person's point of view, the "Civil War", "The War of Northern Aggression", "The War of Southern Rebellion", and other names, but most southerners simply referred to it as "The Wah." Several decades after the conflict, "The Wah" was still a common expression. Some historians believe that it took at least fifty years for the South to recover from this civil conflict. Some others say the South has yet to recover.

In the early days of the Civil War, and even months after South Carolina regained control of Fort Sumter from Union forces in April, 1861, there was very little news that came to Madison County about the war. When news did come, some of it was inaccurate, and it was often embellished. Lee's successes in Virginia and Andrew Jackson's "Stonewall Stand" at the first battle of Bull Run in July of 1861 were well known. The names of Southern generals were a common reference when discussing the battles. Names like Robert E. Lee, Stonewall Jackson, Jeb Stuart, James Longstreet, Jubal Early, John Pelham, Nathan Bedford Forrest, and others were revered and heroic to the Southerner.

Without news media like we have today, accounts from the battlefields came slowly and spotty to those at home. Huntsville was situated on the Memphis-Charleston railroad. This was an important line of transportation to control for both sides. This railway was vital to the South, and Madison County received more news via the railroad about the war than some of the more remote areas.

It didn't take long for the North to realize that the Huntsville Depot on the Memphis–Charleston Railway was about midway of the existing line. The South was busy moving war material and men on the railway to and from the various theaters of the war, so it should have been no surprise when General Ormsby Mitchel marched all night from Nashville, Tennessee to capture and occupy Huntsville.

Mitchel's occupation forces came in the early morning hours of April 18, 1862, and he took the town without firing a shot. The occupation plan was for Mitchel to control Huntsville and its railway junction, thus denying the South this mode of transportation. According to my grandmother, Mitchel's mission was evidently to destroy the public buildings, transportation venues, crops, and food in an effort to "break the will of the people to fight," and he was very good at carrying out this part of his mission.

Mitchel's headquarters were established quickly, and many of the homes in Huntsville's Twickenham district were occupied by his officers. The entire town was under tight Union control. Several public buildings and churches were used in the occupation effort. The nave of the Church of the Nativity on Eustis Street was used as a barn for horses assigned to Mitchel's troops. All of this type of activity in Huntsville had little effect on Isaac Criner's place on Mountain Fork Creek. However, what Mitchel did next would affect and harass the Isaac Criner compound for the remainder of the Union occupation of Huntsville.

In order to destroy as much food as possible, Mitchel sent a contingent of soldiers out daily to destroy crops, stored foodstuffs, and farm animals. The Criner Farm was visited regularly by these dispatched units. Everyone, black and white, went into action carrying out Isaac's defense plan in trying to save the farm animals and food. No one knew how long the war would last, and food, by late 1862, was already scarce. Foodstuffs were at a premium. Butter sold for three dollars a pound; salt, eight dollars a sack; bacon, ten dollars a pound, while cotton dropped to eight cents a pound.

Isaac Criner and his family sought ways to survive in these trying times. Family-owned slaves worked hand-in-hand with family members to survive. Being farmers, the Criners had foodstuffs available; however, after a few Yankee raids, their storehouse of food diminished. To combat the raids, part of Criner's defense system was to post a guard during the daylight hours to watch for the approaching Yankee raids.

A young black boy named Johnny was to give the signal "Yankee's a-coming" whenever a patrol was spotted. The system worked very well, for each member of the household had a duty to perform in hiding food and other items of value. The slave cook, Lily, had a big hoop skirt that had small pockets sewn on the inside into which went the silverware. Johnny was to run the horses to the mountain, and Rebecca was to begin spinning yarn with a spinning wheel on a rug, which was neatly placed over a trap door in the floor where the salt meat was stored. Many precious family stories about these raids and the war years have been passed down through the generations of the Criner family.

On one of these raids, the Yankees found a barrel of sugar hidden in loose cotton in one of the buildings. The soldiers began to dump out the sugar. One of the Criner girls went to the soldier who was scattering the sugar on the ground, looked him straight in the eyes, knelt down, and with her hand, she gathered up loose sugar into her apron. She never broke eye contact with the soldier, and he let her calmly gather the apron of sugar. The family had no choice but to make do with that apron of sugar for the duration of the conflict.

One of the most interesting stories involved the slave boy, Johnny, who was the keeper of the horses. Isaac Criner had one particular stud horse that was special because of his fine qualities. During one Yankee raid, Johnny was too slow in moving the horses to the safety of the mountain and was captured by the Yankees along with this fine horse and a few mares. The Yankee commander took the horse for his personal mount, with Johnny as his groomsman.

This detachment was soon headed north into Tennessee, and Johnny and the stallion saw several battles and skirmishes between the Union and Confederate forces. Johnny recalled several battles but could not recall their names. However, one that he remembered was "The Battle of Nashville." Johnny's duties consisted of caring for the commander's mount, shining boots, and other camp chores. He seemed to get along well with the Union officers and was respectful and obedient.

After the Battle of Nashville, where Union forces had a relatively easy victory while in route to Shiloh, all of the officers proceeded to get drunk. The victory party raged on into the night until the whole Union command fell asleep. Johnny seized this opportunity, saddled the stallion, and rode off into the night toward what he hoped would be Mountain Fork Creek and home.

Traveling by night, asking directions, and telling his story to other Southerners along the way, Johnny gradually made his way south. Directions came hard. However, after many weeks of traveling, he arrived home to a big celebration on Mountain Fork Creek. Isaac Criner described the event of the homecoming of Johnny as parallel to the coming home of the prodigal son in the Bible. They had a big feast of what they had, and all rejoiced at the return of this son who was lost for so long.

Mitchel was relieved of his command in late 1862 because of the rough treatment and the complaints of the civilians in Huntsville. General Nathan Bedford Forrest came through Huntsville in May of 1863 while returning from capturing the Union command of Colonel Abel D. Streight. Streight's raiders made a raid into Alabama as a mounted unit of 2,000 hand-picked troops, and Forrest captured them all with 600 men. Needless to say, Forrest was fast becoming a hero in the eyes of Southerners. Forrest returned from this victory via Huntsville, and he and his men were given a big barbecue celebration. Forrest was awarded the finest horse that could be found in Madison County. Forrest, a farmer from Tennessee, had no formal military training, but he is considered by many historians to be the most dynamic and successful general in the Civil War on either side. (That Devil Forrest/Wyeth)

Criner and his clan continued in survival mode for the duration of the war and coveted any news from the battlefront. The raids continued and most likely were made worse because of the relentless fighting of a Southerner named Milus E. "Bushwhacker" Johnston. Johnston had been a circuit preacher when the war broke out and vowed not to take part in the conflict. He changed his mind when he learned that five innocent farmers on Buck Island, near the town of Guntersville, were merely plowing their fields when they were executed by some of Mitchel's raiders. One wounded man survived after being thrown in the Tennessee River and told of this senseless execution.

After this and other acts of cruelty by Mitchel's Raiders, Johnston became a guerrilla fighter and harassed the command in Huntsville at every opportunity. The Huntsville Union Command thought he had several hundred men in his guerrilla band, but he never had over fifty. Johnston was so talented as a guerrilla fighter that he was never really threatened by the Huntsville Union Command, even though he was their number one enemy target. Most likely, because of Bushwhacker Johnston, Isaac Criner and the entire civilian population of the county received an extra amount of harsh treatment by the frustrated Huntsville occupation forces because they couldn't catch this preacher-turned-soldier that seemed invincible.

Isaac Criner's baby daughter, Martha Woodson, continued her courtship with William Henderson Moore throughout the war years. Moore was a prolific love letter writer and often wrote Miss Woodson, as he called her. (These letters are still preserved in the G. W. Jones & Sons files and provide good reading about portions of the war). Moore was from Lincoln County, Tennessee, and was working as a clerk in a store in Fayetteville when the war broke out. He volunteered in the First Tennessee Regiment with whom he served the entire four years. He must have lived a charmed life, for during these long years he was not once wounded. His first letter of record to Miss Woodson came from Lynchburg, Virginia, dated May 21, 1961. A portion of one of his letters is as follows, copied directly as Moore wrote to his sweetheart:

> Camp 1st Tennessee Regiment
> Between Fredericksburg & Ft. Royal, Va.
> December 19, 1862
>
> Miss Woodson,
> According to your request, I attempt to give you a few items that you may know that I am well and as the boys say about being in a battle, I have "seen the elephant." That is I have been in a fight. And thank God, I came out unhurt, though much of a bargain, as the morning that the battle opened, our Regiment was laying under the heaviest shelling. Major Buchanan, Sawyers, Sanders and myself were lying behind a tree and a bombshell struck the tree about the ground, tearing the tree all to pieces. It wounded all but myself, though stunning me considerable and nearly covering me in dirt. By this

time for two miles in front of us was black with the pomp and splendor of the Federal army and it was the grandest sight I ever beheld. And a frightful one it was, for it seemed to me they had enough to whip the whole world. They came four columns deep in front of us. We were ordered into our ditches and reserve our fire until they got within range and then we turned loose upon them, killing and wounding them almost by regiments until they could not stand it any longer. They broke and all the running they did it. The second column came and we soon put them in a fix for scadadling, and such running was never heard of. Then the third column came and turned a Brigade on our left until the Yankees got in our rear. We began to think we were gone up, but the Bloody 1st never faltering held our position until those on our left received reinforcements and drove the enemy back. Then our whole line charged them about half a mile. They poured shell and grapeshot into us all the time then we fell back to our entrenchments and the way they poured the grapeshot into us wasn't slow. They came as thick as hail. I thought I would never get back to the ditches for I was never as give out as I was. When I got to the ditch, I didn't take time to step into it – I just fell into it and lay there for some time until I got breath. In our company, we lost one killed and two wounded. Major, lieutenant colonel and colonel were wounded. Col. Turney was severely wounded through the head. We lost in the Regiment 49 wounded and six killed. I never saw sutch slaughter, as was on the Yankee side. They were lying in heaps and the field in which they were in caught fire from our shells and the poor wounded Yankees burned to death. Oh, I never saw such a horrible sight in my life. I am thankful that I came out unhurt. We lay under their shelling for three days and nights. If it wasn't for the shelling, I wouldn't mind it so mutch. You must excuse writing, for I have to write on my knee. When I got to camp, the ground was covered with snow and how cold it was. I came very near freezing. We had to lie upon the cold ground and will have to the rest of the Winter. Oh, but we see a hard time indeed. But I can endure it better now than I could last Winter. I hope old J. Johnston will keep the Yankees out of Tennessee and we can hear from each other often. If the Yankees should come into your country and you should leave, you must write immediately. The estimate of the Yankee loss is 18,000 (I think it is that much) and ours wasn't more than 3,000.

W.H.M.

The Union Forces pulled out of Huntsville in July, 1864, with orders to link up with General William T. Sherman as he made his "march to the sea". Sherman's "march to the sea" was an effort to cut the south in two, thus isolating most of Georgia, South Carolina and part of Tennessee. Sherman wanted the Huntsville Union command to cover his rear because he greatly feared Forrest, who was in Mississippi at the time. Before leaving Huntsville, the rear guard of the occupying force was ordered to burn the entire town except for the residences.

 The story goes that the lieutenant left in charge of the burning, burned all the commercial and public buildings. He put off the burning of the Church of the Nativity until last because the rear guard horses were quartered in the nave of the church. It was late in the evening when he was ready to burn the church, but when he raised a torch to burn it, the torch light illuminated the lintel over the door on which is written "Reverence My Sanctuary." Having read this, the lieutenant couldn't bring himself to burn the church so he put out the torch and rode east to catch up with his command and Sherman. This inscription on the lintel of the church can still be seen today.

The South, as well as the whole nation, was greatly relieved on April 9, 1865 when this terrible war finally ended. Robert E. Lee had surrendered to Grant at Appomattox in Virginia, and "Bushwhacker" Johnston surrendered to a Col. Givens on May 11, 1865 in Huntsville. Johnston refused to surrender to a Col. Horner who was the superior officer saying that he "would only surrender to a gentleman." Johnston turned in most of his arms, but he left the best ones hidden in a cave for future use. Many people said that Johnston and his men killed more Yankees and destroyed more war material during the war than any other military unit from Madison County. (Bushwhacker, Johnston/M.E. Johnston)

Southerners buried more people from Madison County in the later 1860s than died during the war, civilian and military. The Southern soldiers returned home in 1864–65 very tired, malnourished, diseased, and maimed only to find a devastated homeland. It would be a long time and several crop years later before a semblance of normal life returned to the South and its people. Even with this period of reconstruction facing Southern people, they were thankful that God had guided this devastating conflict to a conclusion.

William Henderson Moore returned to Mountain Fork Creek after the war and married his sweetheart, Martha Woodson Criner, on October 2, 1865. He made his home on the Isaac Criner farm and lived out his life farming and raising three girls, one of whom was named Elvalena Moore.

Life for those in the South who survived the War Between the States was difficult at best. It has been estimated that the war caused more than 600,000 American men fighting in the war to lose their lives. Eighty-one thousand Alabamians served as soldiers in the Civil War. In Madison County, there were an estimated 400 casualties among men wearing the Southern uniform. By war's end, the Tennessee Valley area of North Alabama was in shambles. Towns such as Bridgeport, Bellefonte, Stevenson, Scottsboro, Larkinsville, Meridianville, Paint Rock, Decatur, Athens and dozens of other small hamlets were virtually destroyed. Huntsville, on the other hand, suffered less damage, primarily because the Union Army had used the town as a base of operations during the occupation. Yankee military personnel had lived in the town's family homes and had used churches and other structures as a part of their garrison. When the final order was given to burn the town only the public and commercial buildings were destroyed, thus saving many of Huntsville's palatial homes. North Alabama, like most of the South, would be re-building until the next century rolled around because of this devastating event. The war consumed the entire nation for four years at the cost of hundreds of thousands of lives and millions of dollars. No one could have predicted the eventual effect on the North or the South, and certainly not the Criners and their extended family living on Mountain Fork Creek.

      The Criner, Moore, and Jones families survived the war and struggled along with other Southern families to put their lives back together. One of the Criner girls observed that she saw more funerals in the first post-war year in Madison County than during the entire four year conflict. Little by little, however, those hardy survivors of the war buried their dead and grubbed out a way of life in the last half of the 19th century. A new South was slowly rising, but it would take another three quarters of a century and two world wars to heal most of its wounds.

The only known image of Milus E. "Bushwhacker" Johnston

Nathan Bedford Forrest

References for this chapter:

"The Sword of Bushwhacker Johnston", M.E. Johnston

Elvelena Moore Jones

"That Devil Forrest", Wyeth

"Incidents of the War", Chadick

Chapter 5 – A New Beginning

Life for the Criners on Mountain Fork Creek was very difficult, as it was with most other Southern families. Gradually soldiers that survived the conflict returned home and worked to make a new beginning for their families. Agriculture was virtually the only economic option available to these families as well as others in the devastated South. Growing corn, livestock, vegetables and cotton comprised most of the effort to scratch out a survival as these families forged ahead.

Many families were not as fortunate as the Criners and their future in-laws. All of the immediate Criner family members returned home from the Great War and began to pick up life as best they could. The future son-in-law of Isaac Criner, William Henderson Moore, returned home and married Isaac's youngest daughter, Martha Woodson Criner. As stated earlier, much of the information from W.H. Moores's experiences in the War was recorded in his letters to Martha. These letters and family research suggest that he fought with the "Fayetteville Guards", a company of the First Tennessee Infantry Regiment. This regiment served during much of the war in A.P. Hill's division, "Stonewall" Jackson's Corps, and the Army of Northern Virginia. Strangely enough, W. H. Moore and a fellow soldier by the name of George Washington Jones served in some of the same military units and fought in many of the same battles. George Washington Jones would later father a son (George Walter Jones) who would marry Moore's daughter (Elvalena Moore) and this union would produce a bevy of Joneses that would have a significant influence on Madison County and the State of Alabama.

Limited information on W. H. Moore exists, either of his private life after the war or as a confederate soldier. This store keeper from Fayetteville served with the First Tennessee Infantry Regiment and most likely served alongside the Fourth Alabama Regiment Volunteer Infantry C.S.A. These military units saw early combat as they proceeded immediately to Virginia in 1861. The Fourth Alabama fought with great distinction throughout the entire conflict: First and Second Manassas, Seven Pines, The Wilderness, Spotsylvania, First and Second Cold Harbor, Boonsboro Gap, Sharpsburg, Gettysburg, Chickamauga, and several other skirmishes. The Fourth Alabama was present at Appomattox on Palm Sunday of 1865 when General Lee surrendered to General Grant. Most likely the First Tennessee and the Fourth Alabama fought alongside each other in many of these battles. Whether W. H. Moore and George Washington Jones ("Wash" as he was called) were known to each other during the conflict is not known. After the war W. H. Moore returned home, married Martha Woodson Criner on October 2, 1865, raised his family, farmed on the Criner farm, and lived in Madison County until his death on June 8, 1904.

Conversely, a great deal is known about Wash Jones and especially his whereabouts during the war. Wash was a member of the Fourth Alabama Regiment Volunteer Infantry C.S.A. (Captain Egbert J. Jones, Huntsville Guards) and served as the unit's Quartermaster. Personal letters from fellow soldiers and excerpts from publications such as "The Huntsville Democrat", "The Southern Advocate" and diaries that survived the war furnish a detailed record of the Fourth Alabama.

The Huntsville Guards responded to the call of duty in March of 1861 following the succession of the State of Alabama in January of 1861. By May of that same year the newly formed Fourth Alabama rendezvoused in Dalton, Georgia ready for departure to Virginia in what was supposed to be a "ninety-day war". Also included in "The Huntsville Democrat" announcement of the rendezvous at Dalton was the fact that Wash had been appointed assistant quartermaster of the Fourth Alabama and elevated to the rank of captain.

Wash served the entire war as a quartermaster for the Fourth Alabama, as it was engaged in the aforementioned battles. Since he was a quartermaster, he was often away from some of the front lines procuring clothing, arms, and material for the soldiers he was supplying. Sometimes he found it necessary to buy shoes and other quartermaster supply items with his own money. Another duty that fell upon Wash was that of informing families of the death of soldiers serving with the Fourth Alabama. One of these tributes was for the death of Commander, Col. Egbert J. Jones, who died from mortal wounds received in battle on September 21, 1861. Wash's report (according to family member Douglas Jones) stated that "Col. Jones was among some of the first men who left their homes to defend the soil of Virginia. He has been one of the first to give his life in that cause."

In June of 1862, Robert E. Lee changed the name of the Confederate forces in Virginia from the "Army of the Potomac" to the "Army of Northern Virginia", a name which stuck for the rest of the war. By October 1862, Wash received a promotion to Major, a rank he maintained until the end of the conflict. In all, the Fourth Alabama was involved in 28 engagements during the war. The war had claimed 939 casualties of the once proud unit called the Fourth Alabama Volunteer Infantry C.S.A. Wash Jones was mustered out of Confederate service from Montgomery, Alabama in May of 1865.

He returned home that same year to his wife Maria Gay and they immediately started to try to put their lives back together. Wash was a principal in the purchase of the Huntsville Hotel which he operated after the war. His son, George Walter Jones, was born on June 22, 1866 in that same hotel. Wash lived only two years after the war, dying on March 11, 1867, apparently from pneumonia brought on by his participation in fighting a local fire during inclement weather.

These two soldiers, George Washington Jones and William Henderson Moore, were part of a legacy that would propagate other offspring to follow in their shoes. Their children would marry, George Walter Jones and Elvalena Moore, and from that union six children would be born that would carry on many of the attributes of the pioneer Isaac Criner. Somehow the pioneer spirit and the hard work ethic of Isaac Criner extended from generation to generation. The children of G.W. and Elvalena Jones, much like the Criners, would face in their time two world wars, a depression, and many other life difficulties. Someone has said that every generation must earn their way amid the difficulties of life presented in their time. Future generations of the Criners were and are destined to struggle with the challenges of life but few, if any, will have a more severe struggle than those who endured the Civil War. The next generation would win and endure World War II and be called "the greatest generation". History tells us that one of the more trying times for any generation is in the engagement of a war. Every war and its consequences are difficult on those engaged in that conflict. Few, however, will approach the extreme burden on this nation as the Civil War. Our prayer, beseeching God, should be that He will guide the affairs of our nation so that our country will never again engage in such a devastating conflict.

Major George Washington Jones' Coat on display at the Civil War Museum near Clanton, Alabama

References for this chapter:

Notes on Wash Jones by Dr. Douglas Jones

Genealogy research by Kathleen Jones and Polly Gandrud

"From Huntsville to Appomattox", Coles

Chapter 6 – G. W. Jones

George Walter Jones lived most of his young life with his uncle, William Brown Jones, probably because his father had passed away only two years after returning from the war. Uncle Will, as he was called, had a profound influence on G. W. and taught him the trade of land surveying. G. W. excelled in math and found his niche early in life in the civil engineering business. G. W. was a product of both private (Plevena Institute) and public schools. G. W. graduated from Winchester School of Engineering, Winchester, Tennessee in 1886. His early interest in land surveying manifested itself into forming his own engineering and land surveying firm, a business that would last 127 years.

Just as he had come to the rescue of G. W. by practically adopting him as a young man, Uncle Will financially helped establish this new engineering firm. The exact date of the opening of the firm named G. W. Jones Civil Engineering is not known, but the year was 1886. The address was 307 Franklin Street, Huntsville, Alabama in a building that is still owned by family members today. From the beginning, the young engineer and surveyor was a success. Most of his early work related to land surveying and G. W., having grown up under his Uncle Will's tutelage, was much in demand for his services. By this time the Federal government had adopted the U.S. System of Public Land Surveys (PLSS). In this system land is described by Section, Township and Range instead of metes and bounds to control the survey, sale, and settling of the new lands. The territory under the jurisdiction of the Thirteen Colonies at the time of independence did not adopt the PLSS. G. W. not only excelled in land surveying, but expanded the services offered by the firm into abstracting, insurance, and engineering projects that revolved around land ownership. The country was recovering from the Civil War by this time and reveled in the era called the "gay nineties". Commerce was good, the cloud of war and some of its aftermath was fading and life for the present was better for all of America.

      Four years after founding his civil engineering firm, G. W. Jones and Elvalena Moore married on February 12, 1890, and moved to a farm in the Hurricane Creek community of Madison County. Uncle Will had left this farm to G. W. when he passed away. The farm consisted of about 1,000 acres near the town of Maysville. The county was growing as well as the G. W. Jones family. Six children were born into G. W.'s family by 1908. The family plan was to farm, carry on the civil engineering business, build a house, and raise the next generation of Joneses. Since G. W. had the business to run, the duties and management of the farm fell to Elvalena. Evidently, she was very efficient in the farm's management because the farm started showing a profit from the very first year. Possibly being only two generations removed from the hard working pioneer Isaac Criner helped sustain Elvalena during this time.

      During those childrearing years, G. W. constructed with his own hands a rather large house for his family. G. W. would survey all day, often leaving before daylight via horseback or buggy, and then return to the farm and work on the house at night. He would return from his day's work, eat supper, visit and advise with the children, and work on the house before getting a few hours rest. Most of the house construction was done at night with Elvalena holding a lantern for light.

One interesting incident happened about this time with the boys. Like most boys of that day, they all worked on the family farm. Planting, plowing, chopping and picking corn and cotton were a part of the life of every young farm person in that age, unlike today when most of the agricultural work is done by machines. The Jones children worked in the fields along with the rest of the family. One pursuit they all had was picking up arrowheads and other Indian artifacts from the fields. Those artifacts were stored in several large barrels that were in the storm cellar near the barn and house. The barrels were filled to capacity with many fine arrowheads and artifact specimens. It made the day more enjoyable as each boy searched for treasure. The Indians who lived here may have been a part of the Cherokee tribe that inhabited the area in Isaac Criner's day.

One year on the Fourth of July, the Jones boys were attempting to make some fireworks for the occasion. Not having money to buy fireworks, they would soak cloth sacks in kerosene, wrap them in wire and after lighting them, throw them into the air to the delight of all. This went well until one of the "fireballs" fell into the barn and burned it completely up. G. W. was not happy and this practice of making "fireballs" was promptly suspended. Sometime later a new barn was erected but the grading for the new barn covered up the storm cellar and the arrowhead barrels. Try as they might they could not locate the storm cellar. Even after the boys were grown, they went back and searched diligently with drills and probes for those arrowhead filled barrels, but to no avail. Someday someone will discover those buried barrels of Indian treasure and wonder just what some Indian was thinking or planning when he put together all these arrowheads which, by the boys count, numbered in the thousands.

Even though G. W. delved into his engineering business more and more each year, he still retained the love of tilling the soil on his farm. Interestingly, this love of farming has flowed from generation to generation all the way from Isaac Criner to the present time. Isaac came to farm in Madison County in 1805, and every year since that time some member of his extended family has farmed somewhere in Madison County. The demand of the engineering business and the education of their six children necessitated a move of the G. W. Jones family to Huntsville in 1911. The farm was sold and G. W. constructed a new house for the family at the corner of Randolph and White Streets (this homesite was located at what is now the Northeast corner of the Annie C. Merts Center, and before that, Huntsville High School).

During this time Elvalena was busy rearing the five boys and their sister Pauline, in addition to setting up housekeeping in their new home. The lot they had chosen in Huntsville was a rather large one, extending from Eustis Street north to Randolph Street. The love of growing things in the soil never left Elvalena. She planted a large garden complete with vegetables and flowers of all varieties. Neighbors were often the recipients of the produce and flowers grown in her garden. Her favorite flower was the "lily of the valley", a small lily with clusters of white bell shaped blossoms hanging in the center. Rambunctious children were well advised not to get on her lily bed. Elvalena's name by this time had been changed to "Mama" Jones, one that stuck for the rest of her life.

By 1930, the City of Huntsville boasted a population increase to 11,554 and, along with the City, the engineering business was expanding during this time. G. W. Jones received his State Professional Engineer recognition as State of Alabama Registered Engineer Number 297 in 1936. G. W. changed the name from G. W. Jones Civil Engineering to G. W. Jones and Sons, Consulting Engineers: a name that incorporated all of his five sons. All five sons graduated from the University of Alabama. Two of the sons (Carl and Edwin) became Alabama Registered Engineers. One son (Howard) became an Alabama Registered Land Surveyor. Another son (Walter) became a renowned geologist. The remaining son (Raymond) died young, but became an engineer five years before Alabama began registering engineers. Pauline, on the other hand, graduated from the Peabody Conservatory of Music.

One surviving and outstanding attribute of the union between Elvalena Moore and G.W. Jones was their love of hard work and personal sacrifice. "Mama" Jones expended daily an unselfish effort for her family that no one, not even her family, could ever know. G.W. willingly gave the necessary direction and effort for his family by building a family business legacy that would survive over 127 years. This couple persevered in hard times, rolled with life's punches, and raised outstanding children, all of whom graduated from college: a feat that was not a common occurrence at the time. Their children, like their ancestor Isaac Criner, were resourceful and hardworking and had a love of the land that continues to the current families today.

G. W. coined a motto for his firm – "a fair measure for a fair price". This motto somehow has since permeated through the future generations of Joneses, men and women, who desire to work for a living, thus earning what they sow in life.

G. W. Jones in His Office at 307 Franklin Street

References for this chapter:

The Author's Grandmother, Mrs. Elvalena Jones

Huntsville Historical Review 2008

Chapter 7 – The Family of Elvalena and G.W. Jones

Somehow amid all the trials of farming, building a new business, serving as an Alabama State Senator from 1927 to 1931, building two houses, and moving from the farm to town, G.W. and Elvalena raised an outstanding family. Their offspring would have a profound effect on Alabama as well as the nation.

All of the boys would serve in either World War I or World War II, except for Raymond, who died at the early age of 39. They were heavily involved in the National Guard and often attended summer camp exercises together. In the 1920s and 1930s, much of the military training involved horses. The skill came naturally to the Jones' boys, having been raised on a farm. Polo, as well as other games involving horses, were encouraged by the National Guard and enjoyed by the Jones brothers. The training also involved marching drills, road and bridge construction, rifle range and other weapons exercises. They often commented that National Guard camp was like an action filled vacation rather than drudgery. What they didn't know was that at least three of them, Walter, Ed and Carl, would endure the rigors of World War II and put to use this National Guard training. Howard had served during World War I in France and Germany, but still participated with his younger brothers in these pre-World War II National Guard training camps.

Some of their favorite outdoor activities were camping, fishing, and canoeing on the Paint Rock River in the Fall. Stories abound of these trips, the fish they caught and the tents they pitched along the riverbank. One of the stories they often told was of a local man by the name of J.Z. Moore who sometimes joined their camp. Evidently, J.Z. was immune from being painfully burned by fire. The story was that he could drink boiling hot coffee straight from the spout and never flinch. Also J.Z. could rake a hot coal from the fire and hold it long enough to light something else and seemingly without pain. Most of the camping was done near the village of Hollytree in Jackson County, Alabama, which was one of their favorite spots. The fish they most often caught was a small bass called a "red eye". This small bass was an excellent fighter and very tasty when cooked over the campfire. They hunted along the river in the Fall and fished in the Spring and Summer months. All of them had fond memories of the Paint Rock River camping experiences.

The Jones boys at National Guard camp

HOWARD CRINER JONES

Howard was known for his mild manner. He always had a ready smile and they nick-named him "Sheep"; however, as a college football player he was certainly neither mild-mannered nor sheepish. Once while Alabama was playing Georgia Tech, he made the sports page headlines of the Atlanta Constitution by knocking out five Tech linemen. The caption stated "Sheep Wrecks Right Side of the Tech Line". Howard married Kathleen Paul and they made their home in New Market, Alabama on a farm only about 2 miles from where Isaac Criner encamped on Mt. Fork Creek in 1804. Howard's middle name was Criner. During World

War I he served with Company C, 304 Ammunition Train which fought mainly in France and Germany. Upon returning from the war and beginning his family, Howard became an outstanding farmer and a master land surveyor. He and Kathleen had four children. Howard Criner Jones, Junior continued to farm the family land that was once owned by Isaac Criner on Mountain Fork Creek, after serving in World War II. Harvey P. Jones became a well-known architect and historian of American building styles - one whose services were sought by many locally as well as from other cities. Edith Jones Ledbetter became a medical doctor serving the town of Rogersville, Alabama and Lauderdale County. Edith also served in World War II as a Navy Wave. Emily Jones Good was the youngest of the children, and became a physicist who made her home in Las Cruces, New Mexico. Evidently Howard and Kathleen did a wonderful job of rearing their children because they all excelled in life. Each carried on the trait of being hard-working, like their parents and grandparents before them.

RAYMOND WILLIAM JONES

Raymond became the leader of the family outdoor activities and was very active in everything he undertook. Raymond was the one who led the fishing, hunting, and canoe trips for the brothers. His leadership most likely paved the way for his brothers to attend the University of Alabama, as well as all five of them serving in the National Guard. Raymond was a fine officer in the National Guard and soon worked his way up the ranks to commanding officer of the unit. After his death, the National Guard Armory on

South Memorial Parkway was named Fort Raymond W. Jones in his honor and in appreciation for his efforts in organizing Huntsville's first National Guard unit. Raymond was an accomplished polo player and excelled in anything athletic. He was the consummate outdoorsman, hunter, and fisherman. It was Raymond who spearheaded the idea of offering multiple services in the family firm of GW Jones & Sons. Property related services - such as appraisals, abstracts of title, as well as title insurance and farm loans - expanded the family engineering business. Raymond married Irene O'Neill and they had one daughter, Peggy Jones Miller. Raymond died at an early age in life (39) in 1931 from pneumonia brought on by an infection in his left cheekbone which was crushed in a football game during his college years (this injury can be seen in the picture found earlier in this chapter). Ironically sulfur drugs were discovered in 1931 which would most likely have saved his life. The family mourned the death of this outstanding leader of the family business and this exceptional engineer.

WALTER BRYAN JONES

Walter also was quite an outdoorsman, hunter, and fisherman, and was well known statewide. He served in World War I and World War II, the latter as a Lieutenant Colonel in the South Pacific. He served as the first Director of Conservation for the state of Alabama, and was generally recognized as one of the nation's finest geologists. He served as State Geologist of Alabama for over 30 years. He also served as curator of Mound

State Park at Moundville, Alabama. The University of Alabama named their oil and gas board building in his honor following his retirement. After retirement, he consulted regularly with G.W. Jones and Sons concerning geologic and foundational problems. Walter married Hazel Phelps and they had three sons: Nelson, Douglas, and Warren. Nelson gave his life during World War II, in service to this country in 1945. Douglas became a geologist and served as the Dean of the School of Arts and Sciences at the University of Alabama. Warren received a degree in geology, like his father, and served as the manager of the Norton Company in Huntsville, Alabama during his career. Walter had a booming voice and was much beloved by all who knew him. It was this Uncle Walter who was very close to the author of this book. Whether it was hunting, fishing, caving, or researching an archaeological site, we always had a special relationship. Walter was very much like his ancestor Isaac Criner, in that he loved hard physical work. On the day he died at age 82, he spent the morning swinging an ax, cutting a load of firewood.

EDWIN WHITING JONES

Edwin (Ed as he was called), also loved the outdoors, particularly quail hunting, and he raised several exceptional bird dogs. Mostly he concentrated on breeding English Setters of the "Louellen" bloodline and entered several field trial contests with his dogs. Ed also graduated from the University of Alabama with a civil engineering degree while also playing on the football team. Following graduation, he worked in the family engineering firm as a partner until his death in 1956. During World War II he served in Nome, Alaska as a Brigadier General with the National Guard. Ed and Carl had purchased a 2,500 acre farm in 1939, just before being activated for duty in World War II. Upon returning from service at the end of the war in 1945, Ed took a particular interest in the farm and the cattle business. Ed was known as one of the county's best cattlemen and was also instrumental in bringing the pasture grass, "Kentucky 31 Fescue" to Alabama. Ed married Katherine Simmerman, who was a concert pianist and piano teacher. They had two daughters, Nancy Jones Walker and Barbara Jones Schmieder, both of whom followed in their mother's footsteps and were accomplished pianists.

PAULINE MYRA JONES GANDRUD

Pauline, who was nicknamed Polly, was the only daughter of G.W. and Elvalena Jones. Polly developed a love for the piano early in life, and after graduating from high school, she became a piano prodigy student at the Peabody Conservatory of Music in Baltimore, Maryland. Polly used this degree to teach piano and perform recitals after marrying in what had become her hometown, Tuscaloosa, Alabama. Interestingly, she was introduced to her husband, Bennie Gandrud, by her brother Walter Jones while he was serving as State Geologist of Alabama. Polly developed an interest in genealogy along with her sister-in-law Kathleen, Howard's wife, and they pursued this avocation for the remainder of their lives. Polly compiled a census of all Alabama counties for 1830 and 1850, and those records are available for research at the

University of Alabama's special collection library. Polly was awarded recognition for her work by the Alabama Historical Commission in 1978, and a reading room at the University Library was named in her honor in 1994. Polly and Bennie had one son, William Bentley Gandrud, who earned a degree in physics from the University of Alabama and a Ph.D. in physics from Johns Hopkins University. After receiving his education and while working for Bell Laboratories and AT&T, William was instrumental in the original development of today's fiber-optic cable technology. Polly and Bennie lived out the remainder of their lives where they had met and married, in Tuscaloosa, Alabama.

CARL TANNAHILL JONES

Carl, the youngest in the family, graduated from the University of Alabama in 1929 with a Bachelor of Science degree in civil engineering. He served during World War II in Alaska and Europe, and attained the rank of full Colonel. Carl was a dynamic leader who was instrumental in bringing a great deal of industry to Huntsville during the 1950s and 1960s. He was responsible for some intricate engineering design projects, one of which was the Huntsville-Madison County Airport, which was later named the Carl T. Jones Field in his honor. The University of Alabama inducted Carl into the Alabama Business Hall of Fame posthumously in 1983. Carl served as a partner in the firm from 1935 until his death in 1967. Carl married Sarah Elizabeth Bryant, and they had three children: Raymond Bryant Jones, Elizabeth Jones Lowe (known as Betsy), and Carolyn Jones Blue.

As World War II approached, all the surviving sons of G.W. Jones were married and had begun to establish themselves as community and business leaders of extraordinary abilities, in spite of the depression, the lack of business, and other hardships of life. Walter, Ed, and Carl were to be heavily involved in the war, as were grandsons Howard Junior and Nelson, and granddaughter Edith. G.W. Jones would remain in charge of the family firm as the war started, already having been in business for almost 55 years. Even a year before war was declared, the small firm of G.W. Jones and Sons was struggling with a lack of business. Raymond had been gone for eight years, and Huntsville was experiencing only moderate growth. Walter was busy serving as State Geologist for the State of Alabama, and G.W., Edwin and Howard remained in the firm doing property line work and abstracts. Carl had gone to work for the U.S. Forest Service in Knoxville, Tennessee following graduation.

Carl and Edwin decided in 1939 that it was time to introduce new ideas and leadership into the struggling engineering business in an attempt to get things going for the firm. In that year, Carl returned to Huntsville to assist in the firm's engineering activities, and to also join in managing the 2,500 acre farm they had purchased south of Huntsville. They hoped that the farm would produce enough revenue for the family should the engineering firm fail. The 2,500 acre farm was run down and had been on the market for four years. The farm's main dwelling was built in 1823 by slave labor from bricks handmade in the yard. The plan was for Carl, his wife Betty, and their family to move into that house and be on-site managers. Edwin and Carl would spend most of their time in the engineering business and farm on the side.

The farm organization was made up basically of sharecroppers who lived on the place, and who farmed various acreages with teams of mules. At one time there were 26 families and 26 teams of mules working about 800 acres on what is now the Jones Valley farm. Much work was required on the main house, and a lot of early effort was spent trying to make it livable. Mama Jones, Carl's mother, thought it was terrible that Carl would ask his pretty wife to live in such a dump. She was so insistent that she told Betty to simply say "No" to the move. In time, however, Carl prevailed, and the family moved into the big house in the Spring of 1939.

Five months after occupying the farmhouse, Ed and Carl's National Guard unit, the 151st Combat Engineer Battalion, was mobilized in anticipation of the war which was still about a year away. Both Ed and Carl were activated and the trauma to both the firm and family was great. Not only did that disrupt the ongoing engineering and abstract business, but now Betty (a city girl) was left in charge of the farm. Betty knew very little about growing things, but she was a good manager and both boys would later give her credit for holding the farm together during those war years. Both Ed and Carl had their military paychecks sent directly to Betty to help with the finances of the farm. During the war Betty would oversee the growing of crops and livestock, making molasses, selling timber, and many other things necessary to keep the farm intact. Little did any of the family realize that this predicament would last five long years.

Part II

Chapter 8 - Gearing Up For War

The Bible says that there will always be wars and rumors of wars (Matthew 24:6). It has been determined by the University of Oslo, Norway, that there have been more than 14,000 wars since 3600 B.C. Currently, the U.S. Department of Defense has identified 43 combat zones in the world today. Over the course of the past 5,800 years, the world has known peace for less than five percent of that time. These statistics do not reveal the misery that wars have inflicted on wounded soldiers and the civilian population. World War II would also leave, in its aftermath, a lot of pain and life-altering events. Much like the Civil War, World War II would affect almost every American family.

The Japanese bombing of Pearl Harbor motivated Americans to be totally dedicated to winning the war. The Japanese fleet commander, Admiral Yamamoto, was assigned the task to carry out the bombing raids on the peaceful Hawaiian Island of Oahu. After the raid, according to the 1970 film, *Tora! Tora! Tora!*, he said, "I fear all we have done is to awaken a sleeping giant and fill him with a terrible resolve." America was awakened; at no time in our history have we been more dedicated to retaliation towards the enemy that had disturbed this peaceful nation.

The peace of the G.W. Jones family was disrupted along with many other families. Three sons would see combat duty in World War II. Two grandsons and one granddaughter would also serve in the war effort. One grandson, Nelson Jones, would pay the supreme sacrifice for his country, and is buried in an American national cemetery in Margraten, Holland.

At one time, "Mama" Jones had five Blue Star flags and one Gold Star hanging in her window on Randolph Street. This was an outward window display by American families who had loved ones serving in the war. (During the early days of World War I, a Blue Star was used to represent each person, man or woman in the Military Service of the United States. As the war progressed and men were killed in combat, and others were wounded and died of their wounds or disease, there came about the accepted usage of the Gold Star. This Gold Star was substituted and superimposed upon the Blue Star. The idea of the Gold Star was to bestow honor to the person for his supreme sacrifice for his country and to recognize the last full measure of devotion and pride of the family in this sacrifice). I remember accompanying Mama Jones to Harrison Brothers Hardware Store during the war. When she got in line to pay her bill, everyone in front of her stepped aside and invited her to move in front of them. This was their way of recognizing and honoring her as a "Gold Star Mother."

Everyone sacrificed to help in the war effort. Women sold their jewelry to purchase war bonds. Household metal, especially aluminum, was collected at the county seat of every county in the nation. Ration stamps were issued for most everything from gas to nylon stockings, and any extra personal cash was invested in war bonds because, as the government slogan said, "Bonds Make Bombs."

Farmers had a little more leeway with rationing because the country anticipated needing foodstuffs in abundance. All single-family residences with a lot that had vacant space were encouraged to plant a "victory garden." Those gardens added to the food supply in case the country ran out of food on the home-front. One unexpected value of the gardens was the fact that young children learned how to grow corn and other vegetables: an acquired skill that carried on into future years. Very few felt comfortable engaging in leisure activities such as fishing, hunting, or sports activities, because there were men fighting and dying on the front lines.

In addition to growing regular farm produce such as corn, cotton, cattle, chickens, and hogs, farmers also grew vegetables in gardens and named their produce "truck crops," meaning that the produce had to be trucked into town to market. The importance of agriculture was recognized early in the war, as the country's leaders surmised that it would be hard for any hungry country to win a war.

Farmers were allowed to either personally forego the draft call into military service, or to designate someone to stay in their stead to farm their land. These designees remained exempt from the draft, which further highlighted the important role that

American agriculture played in winning the war. Carl and Ed decided to leave the farm and go to war, so they designated a dear friend and employee to represent them and manage the Jones Valley farm in their absence. They named Larkin Battle, a black farm hand as their designee, trusting Larkin to take care of the farm and their family. Larkin, his wife, Mandy, and their little girl, Necy, had moved to the farm a few months earlier. Larkin was in good health and a good manager of men, as well as loyal to the Jones' family and its farm. Mandy became a wonderful cook for Carl's family and remained in that position even after the war until her death. Necy and Lula May (Betty's mother) moved into the big house on the farm during the war as "protection," I suppose. The two of them together might have weighed no more than 200 pounds, but they remained as protectors for those five years of war.

    The morning my dad, Carl Jones, left for the war, he called Larkin and me out to the front gate and said, "I don't know how long this war will last. I have made Larkin my designee to stay here and farm in my absence. By the time I get back, you may be a big boy. In between now and then, you may need a spanking that I won't be here to administer. Your mother and I want Larkin to give you spankings if you need it before I get back. The reason is that you might be too big for your mother to handle. You must remember though, it is not Larkin doing the punishing but your mother and me." Larkin didn't have to spank me but twice during the war, but each time he would say, "Remember now, Bubba, this ain't me, it's your mama and daddy." I could not have had a better disciplinarian than Larkin. We had a special bond and respect between us that long outlasted the war.

One other admonition to Larkin from my dad was that, "No matter how long the war lasts, I want you here when I get back." Five years later when my dad walked up to that same front gate, Larkin greeted him by saying, "Well, Mr. Carl, I's still here." Larkin and Mandy worked for the family and were a wonderful blessing to our lives, both during and after the war and until their death. Necy is still employed by my sister Betsy. The Larkin Battle family was very much a part of our lives, and family decisions always included them. I am so thankful for their place in our lives and in our memories.

Portrait of G.W. Jones

Chapter 9 - 151st Combat Engineer Battalion

The mobilization of a National Guard unit for any purpose sends shock waves throughout the affected communities. Family events, school, work, and every function of the local community is impacted. Such was the case in North Alabama when the 151st Combat Engineer Battalion received orders that their unit was inducted into Federal service.

The date was January 27, 1941, and my father, Carl Jones, was the commanding officer of the 151st. This was almost a year before war was officially declared as the result of Japanese forces bombing Pearl Harbor on December 7, 1941. President Roosevelt proclaimed this day would be a "date that would live in infamy" in the history of America.

Work on the newly purchased Jones Valley farm would have to be put on hold, as well as any new office expansion by G.W. Jones and his sons. The entire organization and family went into a survival mode since the impending war clouded the future. Betty managed the farm with both Carl's and Ed's military pay forwarded to her to pay its expenses and mortgage. Lists of planting dates and things to be done were left to her to accomplish.

During the war years, she depended on Larkin Battle to help her, as well as on advice from other area farmers. Even though Betty was a good manager, she was a city girl and had missed growing up in an agricultural environment. She learned quickly and showed a level of leadership that sustained and preserved the farm during the World War II years.

The first ten days of the mobilization were spent in Huntsville with the surrounding community armory personnel, packing equipment. No one knew just when they would deploy, or where in the world they would be ordered to serve. But, being combat engineers, they knew it would most likely not be in North Alabama. Within a few days, they received orders to move via convoy to Camp Shelby, Mississippi, where they trained, anticipating service in the South Pacific.

The 151st encamped at Camp Shelby for six weeks. During that time, Carl thought it would be a good idea to instruct the men on how to deal with poisonous snakes. To this end, he asked his brother, Walter, to drive over to Camp Shelby from Tuscaloosa, Alabama to give the men a "snake talk." Walter readily accepted the assignment and described, in detail, the four poisonous snakes that live in the South. They are the rattlesnake, the cottonmouth, the copperhead, and the coral snake. Walter ended his talk by telling the men that, "if that beautiful little snake with red stripes over yellow stripes (the coral snake) should bite you, don't go running through the woods like a wild Indian, just calmly sit down by a tree, and it will all be over in a few minutes." After this graphic presentation, the men were especially mindful of snakes and talked about what vipers they might encounter if sent to the South Pacific.

In the fifth week at Camp Shelby, they received orders to convoy to Camp Claiborne, Louisiana, where they engaged primarily in engineering skills training. Intense rifle-range target practice was also very much a part of the Claiborne encampment.

Everyone felt they would eventually be engaged in jungle warfare in the South Pacific, but such would not be the case.

In July 1941, the 151st was ordered to load all their equipment and men on a 58-car train bound for Seattle, Washington. They were directed by the War Department to prepare, as best they could, for deployment in Alaska. The Army had changed plans and diverted the unit from duty in the South Pacific to the Arctic climate of Alaska (typical Army).

Upon arriving in Seattle, they had 36 hours to unload the fifty-eight car train and reload the cargo onto ships. Carl vehemently protested these orders as almost impossible to carry out. He demanded that the dock and warehouse personnel be directed to work full time without any break and that all government "red tape" be waived. The Army agreed and the Alabama 151st Combat Engineer Battalion, including men and equipment, sailed for Alaska on schedule. Alaska was not yet a state in 1941, and military duty there was considered "overseas duty." In light of this, the 151st was the first Army unit deployed overseas in World War II.

The units of the 151st were scattered into five different locations in Alaska. Companies A, B, and C, as well as the medical and headquarters detachments were located in Dutch Harbor, Kodiak, Fairbanks, and Sitka, respectively. Alaska is our largest state, and with its long string of Aleutian Islands, it stretches west between the Bering Sea and the North Pacific Ocean for over a thousand miles. Initially Carl commanded and routinely inspected the 151st until the units were reassigned to local commands, which were more efficient. Carl took over as Post Executive Officer at Fort Greeley on the island of Kodiak. There he was promoted to the rank of Lieutenant Colonel and was in "loose" command of the 151st scattered units. Distance and weather made regular inspections and visits to his units difficult at best.

The overall strategic plan for the 151st was to build roads and airfields to defend the Aleutian chain because the Japanese had already taken the western most islands of Attu and Kiska. Weather was the main deterrent in this effort. My father said that America lost more men to the weather than to the enemy in Alaska. Carl, along with everyone else, constantly fought the quick and vast fluctuations of the tides and weather.

Carl remained on Kodiak Island until the Fall of 1941, when he was appointed to Admiral Rockwell's staff for the Attu Invasion, and was subsequently made Chief of Staff of the Kiska Invasion in the Spring of 1943.

Many interesting stories happened during this time of preparation for the defense of the Aleutian Chain. One night, Carl was awakened about 2 a.m. by a soldier who insisted that he accompany him to the job site of a road being constructed on Kodiak. Carl dressed in his arctic gear and dutifully went to the job site. (Generally, the weather was so cold that the 151st heavy equipment was forced to run 24 hours a day. If the dozers, graders, et cetera, were shut down, they were extremely hard to get running again.) A bulldozer had been clearing a roadbed and had taken the rear end off of a large animal buried in the frozen tundra. Soldiers awaited Carl's arrival, hoping that he would have instructions on just what to do next. Carl quickly surmised that this was most likely a mastodon and directed the men to use picks and shovels to finish uncovering the animal. The animal was indeed a prehistoric mastodon with long, curved tusks of almost 12 feet. A fairly large crowd of soldiers and onlookers had assembled by the time the beast was fully excavated. Carl told the group that if this was peace time, the proper course of action would be to send at least part of the mastodon to the Smithsonian. We were at war, however, and he ordered two things: (1) the meat was fresh because the animal had green leaves in its mouth and was "quick frozen." In lieu of this, chunks of meat from the mastodon were taken to the mess hall and cooked for anyone who wanted to eat it. There were very few tasters, but for those who did, at least they could say they had eaten a prehistoric meal, and (2) the tusks were long and cumbersome, so he had them cut up into 18 inch pieces and gave each officer one as a memento. (I still have his piece in my home).

During this time, U.S. forces were busy building airfields on the western Aleutian Island, and the Japanese were busy implementing an aggressive strategy to dominate the Pacific Theater. In 1942, the primary Japanese objective was the island of Midway. In order to successfully attack Midway, the Japanese planned to create a diversion by bombing Dutch Harbor, Alaska, hoping to draw the U.S. fleet north and out of the Midway area. The U.S. Fleet Commander, Admiral Nimitz, didn't bite on this feint by the Japanese raid on Dutch Harbor and proceeded to win the Battle of Midway, thus turning the tables on Japan, which was an enormous step toward winning the war in the Pacific.

The first Japanese bombing of Dutch Harbor occurred on June 3, 1942. Much like Pearl Harbor, the attack caught U.S. forces by surprise. The enemy controlled the skies for the 20-minute raid uncontested by our fighters. The Japanese only lost one Zero fighter plane, and our casualties totaled 52 soldiers and a lot of damage to our boats, equipment, and supplies.

The second bombing of Dutch Harbor occurred the next day, with the U.S. losing 18 soldiers and thousands of gallons of fuel. Japanese losses were heavy, primarily because our fighters surprised the enemy, attacking them from the airfields on Umnak and Cole Bay (airfields that were constructed by the 151st). Ground fire also thwarted some of the attacks, thanks to defenses set and established by a General Simon Buckner (one of my Dad's friends). At the exact same time of these Dutch Harbor bombings, Japanese Fleet Commander, Admiral Yamamoto, was losing the Battle of Midway. He ordered his forces in Alaska to come to his aid, thus ending the diversion strike against the Aleutians for the time being. The Dutch Harbor attack was a small success for Japan, but it had alerted and strengthened the resolve of U.S. forces in Alaska.

Carl was busy at his home base in Kodiak, managing the reconstruction of Dutch Harbor and making trips to places like Adak, Sitka, Kiska, Attu, Anchorage, Nome, Cole Bay, Seattle, and even San Francisco. In all, Carl traveled almost 46,000 miles by the time he left Alaska in November 1943. Unfortunately, the

U.S. invasion of Attu and Kiska loomed ever closer. Between the bombing of Dutch Harbor and the re-taking of those two islands, Bomber Commander Colonel William Eareckson's planes flew almost nonstop searching for the Japanese fleet. Each day, the reports were "mission without success – unsuccessful search – search results negative," to which Eareckson angrily retorted, "Find the bastards."

While this was going on, there was a lot of down time for the Kodiak-based soldiers as they prepared to fight at some future location. During this time, my father's headquarters received a visitor flown directly from Washington. The visitor was a petite, well-groomed, articulate lady sent by a U.S. Senator to make sure that our soldiers were being treated well. My dad, being too busy to conduct a tour, assigned the lady visitor to the colorful "Squeaky Anderson," who was a local ship commander for the Army. Commander Anderson showed the lady some of the Navy ships and facilities, as well as the Army barracks. At the conclusion of the tour, she leaned close to Anderson and asked in a confidential tone, "Commander Anderson, tell me, what do these men really need and I'll try to get it for them." Anderson didn't hesitate and said, "Madam, what these men really need is about a thousand whores." With this, the Congressional visitor abruptly left and further inquiries ceased for the duration of the war.

In early January of 1943, Carl was promoted to the rank of Colonel and was the engineer coordinator for the Attu attack. Carl subsequently became part of Admiral Rockwell's staff, planning the invasion of Attu. In April of 1943, Carl was reassigned to begin planning for the Kiska invasion under the command of General G.C. Corlett. Carl was eventually made Chief of Staff for the Kiska task force under Corlett. My Dad had great respect for General Corlett, and their relationship would surface again in Europe, as World War II proceeded. The reason the Army switched from invading Kiska to invading Attu, was because fewer ships were needed to take Attu, and because Kiska was heavily fortified with enemy troops and weaponry. Attu had a smaller garrison and was deemed an easier target, so our forces "leapfrogged" Kiska to the outermost island of Attu. This "leapfrogging" maneuver would prove to be successful and was used again later in the Solomon Islands and in Europe. This would be the first amphibious mission by the U.S. in World War II, and they did it using air support from airfields built by the 151st.

Admiral's Staff, Adak, Alaska (Carl Jones in Center), November 1943

Carl "Sourdough" Jones, Kodiak, Alaska, December 1941

Chapter 10 - Attu

Attu is the western-most island of the Aleutian Island chain, which is the world's longest archipelago. Bounded on the north by the Bering Sea and on the south by the North Pacific Ocean, the islands are recipients of icy, cold winds from Siberia that blow south across the Bering Sea and collide with the warm Japanese Current flowing north. The two clash at the Aleutian Island chain, forming around-the-clock storms with winds up to 140 mph. Fog regularly deters shipping and air travel. The Aleutians are one of the only places in the world where wind and fog occur simultaneously. In a normal year, the Western Aleutians have only 10-12 days of clear weather.

Distance, as well as weather, was another severe factor in the invasion of Attu and Kiska. Attu is five time zones from Alaska's capitol city of Juneau (about the same distance as from Atlanta to San Francisco). Any military battle plan is difficult, but this one was much more difficult due to those circumstances. Under General Simon B. Buckner's dogged leadership of his combat engineers (some of which were the 151st), landing strips on six Aleutian Islands – Umnak, Adak, Amchitka, Kiska, Shemya, and Attu were constructed before World War II ended. The war in the Aleutians has been called "Buckner's War" by some and the "1,000 Mile War" by others.

I'm sure that when Secretary of State William H. Seward signed the purchase agreement with Russia in 1867 to acquire Alaska, he had never even heard of Attu. The seven million dollars the U.S. paid for Alaska was well worth the price. Most of Alaska is rich in wildlife and natural resources and, unlike the Western Aleutians, it is mostly habitable. One U.S. commander was quoted as saying, "Why would anyone, other than the Aleuts, even want to occupy these inhospitable islands?"

Despite such hardships, the Battle of Attu began on May 11, 1943. This was to be a U.S. Army Infantry amphibious landing, the first one in Army history. The U.S. assault troops planned to make shore landings in Massacre and Holtz Bays (Massacre Bay was named by the Aleuts in the Eighteenth Century, reflecting the annihilation of the natives by the Russians). After considerable delay, primarily fog related, the first salvo was fired just after 6 p.m., and the Battle of Attu was on.

First, the beaches of Massacre and Holtz Bays were to be secured, and then U.S. forces began moving men and equipment inland. The occupying Japanese forces were all established on the ridges overlooking these beaches and landing sites. For a period of time, the Japanese seemed content to stay put in the hills and allow U.S. forces to land men and equipment. (A copy of the battle plan for progress beyond the beaches to take Attu was recorded in Carl Jones' journal, and is included at the end of this chapter).

The Battle of Attu was estimated by General DeWitt to be a three-day operation. Very little goes as planned when involved in a war, however, and such was the case at Attu. The soft terrain of muskeg in the arctic tundra inhibited forward progress beyond the occupied beaches. The 20-foot tide fluctuations, as well as the cold, rainy weather, inhibited air support and the soldiers' clothing and boots were much too light for the Aleutian Islands. Wheel-driven vehicles were useless and storm-related radio static limited communications. Fog limited the observance of the enemy on the high ground above the beaches. However, the Japanese could see movement of the U.S. forces by looking down through the fog. In all, the Battle of Attu lasted for 19 torturous days, with much of the fighting occurring hand to hand.

The final battle ended on May 30, 1943, with the annihilation of Japanese Commander Colonel Yasuyo Yamasaki's surviving force, as he made a suicide charge against more numerous U.S. forces. Japanese soldiers who had fought so hard for Attu mostly committed suicide in the end. (See picture at the end of this chapter.) After the battle, American burial parties counted 2,351 Japanese bodies, mostly killed by clutching suicide hand grenades to their chests. Only 28 Japanese prisoners were taken alive, and none of them were officers.

American losses were 549 dead, and 3,829 combat casualties, a number of which were severe weather injuries, mostly frostbite and trench foot. U.S. soldiers who died on Attu were buried in collective graves of eight on this God forsaken island called Attu.

The painful lessons learned at the battle of Attu influenced the upcoming Kiska Campaign and other campaigns throughout the war. One vital lesson was to issue proper clothing for the foot soldiers. Important changes in foot gear, clothes, tents, bedrolls, and food were made and most probably saved thousands of soldiers from weather-related injury in the European Theater, as well as in other conflicts. The battle also highlighted the fact that air support for any type of combat invasion was of utmost importance (at one point during the battle of Attu, Eareckson's aircraft were stymied because of poor visibility and circled the island at 20,000 feet for five days). Another brutal realization was the tenacity of the Japanese soldiers – they would fight to the death with no thought of surrender.

Throughout the Attu conflict, the 151st men and equipment were attached to the other engineer units supporting infantry troops. The 151st had men and engineers that were involved with beach supply and unloading control, as well as those trying to build roads inland. They were involved in several skirmishes in the 19-day invasion. The most significant battle for some of the 151st men was when they joined the 50th Engineers, which happened to be with the unit that stopped Yamasaki's final and fatal charge. The 50th Engineers were given credit for standing firm in the face of the final assault. Their stand prevented the Japanese from capturing U.S. artillery pieces, thus dealing a final blow to the enemy. After the battle, one of the hills in this engagement was named "Engineer Hill."

Carl Jones, along with most of the Kiska task force, had remained aboard the USS Battleship Pennsylvania during the battle, supplying logistical command information and coordination for the mission. Carl had already been reassigned to the Kiska task force, and his observation of the Attu campaign would be valuable in the future. Kiska was the next objective in this 1,000 Mile War, and the planning for that attack would be greatly influenced by the

Battle of Attu. This battle on the wind-swept island of Attu didn't receive much historical or media coverage, but it is ranked as the second most costly battle in the Pacific Theater in World War II, second only to Iwo Jima.

Massacre Bay Beach

Engineer Bulldozer Stuck in Muskeg

over 1000 bodies in this area. The nip in the foreground Committed Suicide with hand grenade

Over 1,000 Japanese Bodies, Mostly by Suicide

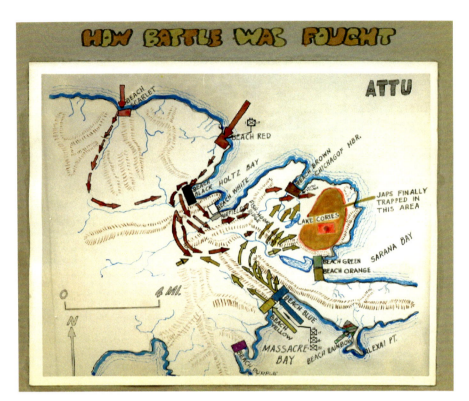

How the Battle Was Fought

Chapter 11 - Kiska

The initial interest of the Japanese in the Western Aleutian Islands probably was due to their close proximity to Japan's Kurile Islands. The Kurile Islands were home to a huge Japanese military base called Paramushiro, which was the headquarters for Japan's northern command. Paramushiro was within air range of future potential airfields that would be built by U.S. forces on Adak, Amchitka, Shemya, Kiska, and Attu. The Japanese strategy was twofold: to defend their facilities in the Kurile Islands; and offensively, to make another step toward the invasion of Dutch Harbor, Anchorage, and possibly even the U.S. Mainland.

Prior to the invasion of Kiska, the U.S. command ordered a raid on Paramushiro – which was very successful. The raid caught the Japanese base by surprise, and while the damage inflicted to ships and infrastructure was not devastating, it made a resounding statement that the Imperial Nation of Japan could be reached by land bombers. This was the first land-based bombing raid on Japan in the war. Other bombing raids were implemented after this one on the Kurile Islands, but they were not as effective. The valuable strategy was to keep the Japanese engaged defensively while the Kiska invasion was being implemented.

During the same time period of the Kurile raids, an almost impenetrable Allied blockade of Kiska was put in place. U.S. Intelligence had established the fact that the Japanese strength on Kiska was formidable. An estimated 6,000 soldiers were dug in, with fortifications and living quarters much superior to that of the

Attu occupation. So the Kiska invasion command, of which Carl Jones was a member, made an intricate plan of attack to retake the island. The invasion was to occur in the second week of August, 1943. Prior to this, in the 3rd week of July, air strikes and naval bombardment began, as scheduled.

In less than an hour after U.S. naval forces had begun shelling Kiska, the blockade and shelling forces received orders to leave the Kiska effort and sail southwest, to intercept approaching enemy ships. Seven blips on radar screens from at least four different Allied sources reported these alarming radar images. The projected course of the blips put them in a direct line to Kiska. Reluctantly, the admirals of the Allied ships left the Kiska effort and pursued the reported sightings. The phantom blips never materialized into being real enemy ships, however. And even after the war, neither Japanese nor Allied intelligence could offer an explanation. Of course, radar, at that point in time, was in an elementary stage of development. Whatever the reason, the phantom radar blips afforded the Japanese forces on Kiska a unique opportunity – one of which they took full advantage.

The Japanese high command at Paramushiro decided to evacuate Kiska, rather than repeat the devastating losses at Attu. There were no Japanese surface ships available for the evacuation, however, so the high command sent a fifteen-ship submarine convoy under the command of Admirals Kawase and Kimura, to evacuate the 5,183 defenders from Kiska. Five of the submarines rammed one another in the fog, damaging two of them so badly that Kimura sent them back to Paramushiro.

During the night of July 27th, the remaining subs rendezvoused with their oiler and refueled. Being only 50 miles southwest of Kiska, shortly before noon on July 28th, they made a run through a light fog for the island, unaware that the Allied blockade was chasing the phantom blips. The Japanese garrison on Kiska was ready and had been ready for some time. They had set demolition charges, booby traps, and destroyed their supply dumps in an effort to leave nothing of military value for their enemy.

Kimura, because he was two submarines short, ordered the men to leave everything behind except their personal belongings. Hundreds of small arms, rifles, and automatic weapons were cast into the shallow water near the docks. In less than an hour, the total Japanese force on Kiska (5,183 men), climbed aboard eight of the submarines. The enemy left Kiska Harbor at 7:30 p.m. and was 200 miles out to sea by dawn. Admiral Kawase and his command had pulled off one of the war's most daring maneuvers without firing a shot. The possibility that his fleet's approach toward Kiska might have caused the radar blips was never determined, but remains as a possible cause of the "mystery of the blips."

Unaware of the unconventional evacuation, Allied forces continued to pound Kiska. The battleships and destroyers assigned to the blockade returned from chasing the phantom blips and continued their bombardment of Kiska. Aircraft continued bombing runs, but gradually something appeared abnormal. The pilots reported seeing no humans at all, only dogs roaming aimlessly around the island. Bomb craters were not being filled between raids. There was no anti-aircraft fire or smoke from previously occupied structures. Colonel Eareckson's planes even dropped surrender leaflets on Kiska, but there was nobody there to read them. General Buckner was very suspicious that the enemy had evacuated. General DeWitt thought that enemy was there and had holed up in tunnels awaiting the invasion. Finally, Admiral Kirkland made the decision to proceed with the troop landing, stating that, "if the enemy was not there, then at least this would be a good training exercise."

August 15th was D-day, and the Allied assault troops were loaded into the unstable LSTs. Because of the ever present rough weather and raging seas, troops were seasick before reaching the beach. The aircraft strafing continued ahead of the assault troops, against what was eerily becoming a phantom enemy. Some 35,000 Allied combat soldiers were deployed across the deserted island of Kiska. There were 313 Allied casualties, mostly from friendly fire caused by shooting at each other in the fog. Corlett said that he was "tickled pink that we didn't have to fight for the island." Almost immediately, Corlett converted his landing force into a construction crew. Amazingly, in less than two weeks, engineers, including some of the 151st men and equipment, had an operating airfield on Kiska. The invasion planners had expected heavy casualties in taking Kiska; one of the relieved commanders said, "That stinking island is not worth one single life."

The invasion of Kiska marked an end to the Aleutian Chain Campaign. Earlier, the Navy expected 5,000 deaths would be necessary in retaking the Island of Kiska, which had no real strategic value.

The following, copied directly from Carl Jones' journal, is his description of the conclusion of the Aleutian Campaign after the invasion of Kiska:

> "With the departure of the last Japanese from Kiska, the Aleutian Campaign may be said to have ended. But there was no cessation of the arduous, unspectacular effort, which had brought success after nearly 15 months. The bitter battle against the weather went on as usual. Bases still had to be completed, air facilities had to be improved and expanded for expected operations against the Kuriles in the future.
>
> The anticlimactic character of the invasion of Kiska, while disappointing because our forces, well-prepared at the least, were prevented from coming to grips with the enemy, were nevertheless compensated by lives saved and lessons learned under conditions which were nearly those of combat. The withdrawal of the Japanese without a fight was unfortunate in one sense. In another sense it presented us with a false picture of what might be expected from the enemy when the odds were hopelessly against him. Instead of fighting to the death, as at Attu, they faded into the fog without a

struggle. But Attu and not Kiska, was to be the pattern of the future."

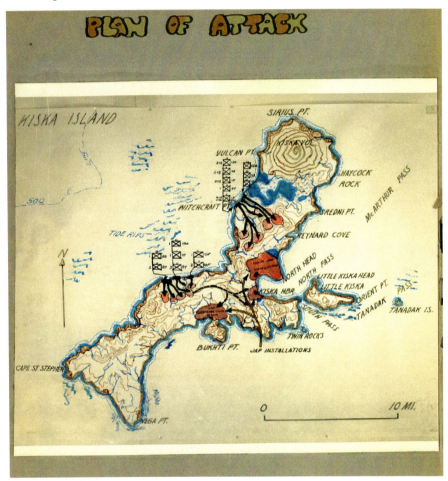

Kiska Plan Of Attack

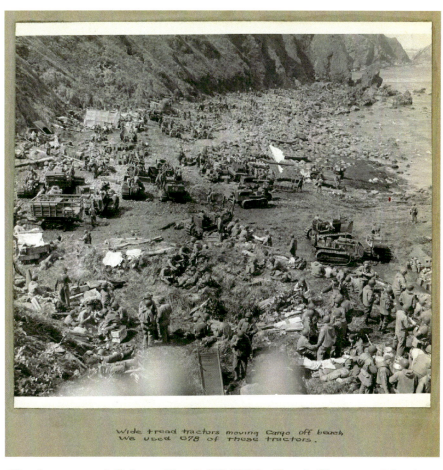

Wide tread tractors moving cargo off beach. We used 678 of these tractors.

Engineers and Others Used 678 Wide Track Tractors Moving Cargo Off the Beach

underground shelter passageway - Japs had underground living space for 20,000 -

Japanese Tunnel, Kiska

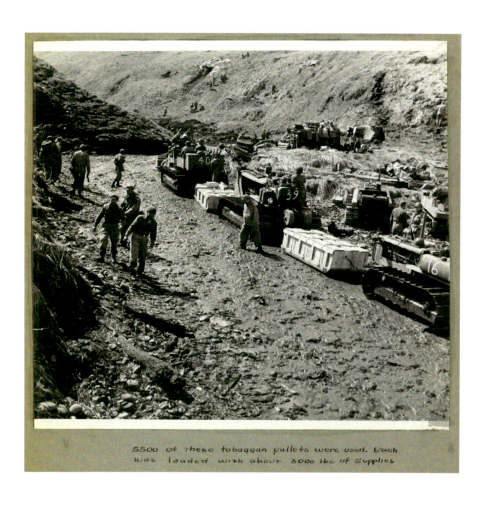

5,500 Toboggan Sleds Were Used To Move Supplies Inland. Excellent Muskeg Transportation

Chapter 12 - More Alaskan Experiences of Carl Jones

"The Dummy City"

Early in the Alaskan deployment the decision was made to build a dummy city as an exact duplicate of the Kodiak Island base. The thinking was that, if the Japanese were to send bombers to bomb this important base on Kodiak Island, they would bomb the dummy city instead. The location was 20 miles short of the base on an uninhabited island in a direct line between Paramushiro and the Kodiak base. The dummy city was to be lighted with strings of light to the exact dimensions of the base at Kodiak. The 151st was given the task of landing on the island and erecting the city. My father accompanied this task force in December of 1941. He and his men boarded an icy Landing Ship, Tank (LST) and made a rough trip to the island.

Construction of the dummy city was expected to last ten days. The task force loaded generators, building supplies, and provisions for the men to complete the work. One thing they underestimated was the tide fluctuations of up to 20 feet. They reached the uninhabited island shortly after noon but could not get within 100 yards of the shore. The water was waist deep when the LST door was lowered and ready to unload. Having no other choice, my Dad, along with his men, jumped into the water and carried the tools, material, and equipment to the beach on their shoulders. This took several hours and had to be finished in the dark. Some tents with generators were quickly erected for the men so that they had a place to dry off and warm up from the frigid waters of the Pacific Ocean. The LST left and returned to the Kodiak base with instructions to return in ten days.

Fortunately, the weather was reasonable, and construction proceeded as planned. The LST reported back to the island in ten days, but because of the foul weather, could not even get close to the beach. The temperature had dropped, so the decision was made to wait a few days and hope that the tide conditions and weather might improve. It took an anxious three weeks before conditions improved sufficiently to leave the dummy city island.

During the long three week wait, food ran low and no resupply was in sight. Fortunately, the group had two 12-gauge shotguns and a case of shells, along with four .22 caliber rifles. The guns were given to the medics who were instructed to shoot snowshoe rabbits and ducks. For almost three weeks, the dummy city construction crew subsisted on fire-roasted duck and rabbit. The Lord provides generously for those who help themselves to His bounty.

The only named part of the uninhabited dummy city island is a place called Middle Bay. In the group that built the dummy city, there were two locals named Tom Felton and a fisherman by the name of Rocky Rothwell, both of whom were familiar with Middle Bay. They were included in the construction group because of their knowledge of the island. Rothwell fished its shores regularly and Felton came there to hunt brown bear. My dad, being a hunter himself, was very fond of Tom. Tom was part of the party that killed an 1,800 pound bear (pictured at the end of this chapter) that is now displayed at the University of Alaska in Fairbanks.

THE BEAR ATTACK

During the construction of the dummy city, an interesting event occurred. The survey party was to lay out the dummy city and also survey an alternative site some distance away for the maintenance crew attending the generators. The survey was going well; they posted a man ahead of them armed with an M1 rifle to watch for bears. My dad was near the transit making notes when they heard nine shots in rapid succession coming from the lead man. Immediately, they retrieved their weapons and rushed forward to check on him and the source of the shots. When they arrived at the scene, they found a very scared soldier in a small Aspen tree with a tremendous brown bear chewing at its trunk. The bear had obviously been in a killer mode, but he was near death, having been shot repeatedly. The soldier had done as he was trained and put a neat pattern of nine shots in the bear's chest. Of course, these were military rounds that would go all the way through the bear's body with very little shock or damage. Hunting rounds usually have lead points which are much more effective. The soldier said that the bear attacked him without warning, so he fell to one knee and fired nine shots into the beast. When he ran out of ammunition, he ran to the nearest Aspen tree and climbed it shouting prayers aloud as he went. When asked what he prayed for, he said "I asked the Lord to help me, but if he wouldn't help me, please don't help that bear either."

The bear was very large, but with no scales available to weigh him, his weight remains unknown. Tom Felton said that he was comparable to the bear that is mounted at the University of Alaska in Fairbanks. Fortunately, no damage was done by the bear, except to the Aspen tree, and the survey was eventually completed. After this instance, they posted two men with rifles just in case the survey party was attacked again. The brown bear is one of only three wildlife species in the world that has no fear of man and will attack unprovoked.

The weather eventually cleared, and the LST picked up the men directly from the beach. The dummy city was never bombed but served as a decoy in case of an attack. Fortunately, Alaska teems with an abundance of wildlife. Every man was most thankful to be sent to Alaska rather than the South Pacific. Years later, after the 151st had returned to Alabama, their colorful war stories revolved around Alaska's breathtaking beauty, unpredictable weather, and bountiful wildlife.

ED JONES

Carl's brother, Edwin Whiting Jones, was also deployed to Alaska at this time with the same National Guard activation. Ed's primary base of operation was in the Cold Bay and Nome, Alaska areas. Ed rose to the rank of Brigadier General, the highest rank of any of G.W. Jones' sons, and he was particularly well known in the Nome area. According to Carl's journal, they had a chance to visit together at Cold Bay on April 15 and 16, 1942. Other than that visit, nothing is recorded of their contact with each other, except by way of mail and an occasional telephone/radio contact. Ed served out the war in Alaska and fell in love with the area and its wildlife. Ed, like his other brothers, was an avid hunter and fisherman. He particularly liked to hunt the Alaskan Ptarmigan, which reminded him of the southern bobwhite quail that he had often hunted in Alabama with his family.

It has been said that war makes a more dramatic change in a country and its people than any other event. Certainly this has been true in the life of this country. The most dramatic change for our country was the Civil War, and I'm sure a close second would be World War II. I'm positive that Isaac Criner could never have dreamed that five of his great-grandsons would fight on foreign fields so far away from Madison County. The price of any war is high, particularly to families like ours who had so many involved and so many at risk.

UMNAK

As Allied forces moved westward out the Aleutian chain of islands, one of their more important bases was Dutch Harbor. This island has an excellent harbor and is very popular today as a fishing harbor. The hit show, *Deadliest Catch,* a TV series on commercial fisherman, bases its episodes out of Dutch Harbor. The airfield at Dutch Harbor was originally constructed by the 151st combat engineers from the Huntsville, Alabama area.

West of Dutch Harbor about 100 miles is an island named Umnak. While not a big step toward Attu and Kiska, it was nevertheless a strategic move in the right direction. There was a diversity of opinion among Allied leadership as to whether Umnak was worth any effort. While the dialogue among the leadership was progressing, one of the leaders asked the 151st to make a surveillance trip to the island for more information. Since it was not a priority, my dad told the company commanders to ask for volunteers to make the reconnaissance trip to the island. The commanders had difficulty getting any volunteers, but finally were able to assemble about fifteen men for the job. The trip was made and the usual comments about docking sites, possible airfield locations, and the like were reported. Another trip to the island was subsequently planned, and again the plea for volunteers went out. Almost immediately, over 100 men volunteered for the trip. The commanders were suspicious as to why so many would volunteer. When the third trip was announced, the volunteers numbered over 200. The mystery was finally solved when it was learned that the island of Umnak had no men on it at all, only women. Evidently, all the native men were gone on an extended fishing trip.

THE TRAIN TRIP

In the Spring of 1943, Carl traveled to San Diego, California, and for about eight weeks he worked on the logistical plans for the Attu and Kiska invasions. Seizing the opportunity, he asked Betty to travel from Alabama by train to San Diego. In a time of war, one never knows when the last opportunity to see your family will occur. Train reservations could not be made because traveling servicemen had priority seating over civilians.

Nevertheless, Betty quickly made the decision to make the trip and to take Betsy and me with her. I was seven, and Betsy was three years old.

We boarded a train in Decatur, Alabama, and headed west to see our beloved father. Things went pretty well until we got to Houston, Texas. When we attempted to change trains, the conductor informed my mother that the train was full of troops and had no seats available. She argued and tried everything she could to get us on the train, but to no avail. In despair at being trapped in the train station for possibly days with two small children, she sat down on her suitcase and began to cry. Betsy and I lingered nearby, not knowing what to do. An Army Colonel came by and asked my mother what was wrong. Betty tearfully explained that she was en route to see her husband in San Diego, and it would be several days before another train was available. This Colonel immediately took charge of the situation telling my mother to get her things and her children and to take his arm and accompany him back to the train. He walked up to the conductor and demanded a place on the train for his "wife and children." The conductor informed him that he would be glad to accommodate the family, but there was not one seat left. The Colonel would not be deterred and asked if anyone was riding in the women's restroom. "No, sir," the conductor replied. "Then put my family in there until El Paso, and then some seats should be available," said the Colonel. The conductor complied, and my mother hugged the Colonel, greatly relieved. So I rode sitting on a trashcan with my head against the sink all the way to El Paso, while mother and Betsy lay on a blanket draped over some luggage on the floor. Afterwards, we never again saw the Colonel that helped us that day. He just faded away into the large crowd of soldiers in the busy train station. Sometimes in life we encounter angels unaware, one of which he surely must have been.

    The rest of the trip was somewhat uneventful. I remember crossing the desert, and since the train was not air-conditioned, we used wet handkerchiefs to keep our mouths from becoming so dry. One other incident I remember was, one morning, several soldiers came by and asked my mother if they could take Betsy to the dining car for breakfast. She agreed, and Betsy, at the ripe old age of three, had her first date. The soldiers came back laughing and thanking my mother for letting her go with them. Like most soldiers, I think they must have missed being with children and being at home. Betsy was a very cute blond-headed little girl, and she had surprised them all by ordering sauerkraut and buttermilk for breakfast. You can take the girl out of the country, but you can't take the country out of the girl.

    We enjoyed the visit with my father in San Diego. It was our first trip to California. We swam in the cold Pacific Ocean, went to Balboa Park Zoo, and stayed with him for about ten days until he had to return to Alaska. The train trip home was easier, since most of the troops were being sent West. We had sleeping berths most of the long way home, which was much more comfortable. Looking back, it was very courageous for my mother to take a seven-year-old boy and a three-year-old girl on a train across the United States without guaranteed reservations. When we did arrive back home to the farm, we were most thankful for the safe trip and for the chance to see my father again. We appreciated every prayer that had been uttered by those at home for us and our loved ones fighting so very far away.

Tom Felton, Tom Nelson and two Soldiers Middle Bay 1943. This kodiak bear weighed 1800 lbs was killed 200 ft. back of Tom Felton house

The Bear Attack

Ed being decorated with the Legion of Merit medal, Nome, 1944

Chapter 13 - Change of Venue

By the end of the Summer of 1943, Allied forces ceased to harass and bomb Paramushiro, as well as other nearby Japanese installations. The fighting in Alaska had mostly come to an end, except for keeping watch on the enemy to prevent another "Pearl Harbor" style surprise attack by the Japanese. The 151st men and equipment were kept busy on construction projects, and a significant quantity of installation improvements was undertaken. Across the Pacific Ocean, however, the war was raging, and the war in Europe was also heating up, especially in Italy and Northern Africa.

In the Fall of 1943, Colonel Carl T. Jones received an unusual communique relieving him of all of his current duty in Alaska. The memo said that a plane would pick him up in three days and fly him to Washington, D.C. Carl was bewildered and confused by the order, and pondered over and over as to whether he had "messed up" any of his assignments. In three days, a P-38 fighter plane came to Kodiak and picked up Carl and all his belongings. En route, they stopped in Seattle to refuel, where Carl called Betty and said that he had talked the pilot into landing in Huntsville for the night. Carl told her to gather all the family and friends she could, because they would only be able to stay for about eight or nine hours. The P-38 landed in Huntsville about 8 p.m., and was gone by the next morning. Nobody slept that night; family and friends excitedly came and stayed until it was time for him to leave. A large number of black families, particularly the men from the farm, also came by to see Mr. Carl, their hero. They hadn't seen him in almost four years, but I think to them he represented not just a soldier fighting for our country, but someone fighting for *them*, the farm and their way of life. The P-38 left Huntsville early the following morning bound for Washington, D.C.

After arriving in our nation's capital, Carl reported to the Army-Navy Staff College and learned that he was to teach amphibious landing procedures for a minimum of two weeks. Armed with this information, he called and asked Betty to drive to Washington, along with Betsy and me, and to stay as long as he was on this assignment. Betty immediately gathered all the ration stamps she could find from the farm, friends, and family. Gas, oil, tires, and the like had to be purchased with ration stamps and it seemed there were never enough. Since there was no interstate system and very little road network at all, careful planning had to be made to insure that there would be gas available for the trip. Our car was a black '39 Pontiac sedan, and Betty drove all the way. The trip took two days and really went pretty well. The biggest mechanical fear was a flat tire. I was only nine, but the men on the farm carefully taught me how to fix a flat tire and pump the tire back up by attaching an air line to one of the spark plug inlets. I had the procedure "down pat," but fortunately we went without a flat tire for the entire trip.

My father had rented an apartment at the Francis Scott Key apartment complex, which was very comfortable. He was busy during the day at the Staff College, often teaching amphibious landing procedure eight to ten hours a day. At night, even though he was tired, we attended events in the Washington area. When he was able during the day, we visited the Smithsonian and other museums. We even rode the paddle boats on the Tidal Basin and climbed the stairs in the Washington Monument. One night, Carl came in about 8 p.m., ate supper, and announced that he was being shipped out the next morning. He didn't know where he was going but had orders to be at the airport ready to leave by 5 a.m.

Later the next day, we started back to Alabama, the farm, and home. Lula May Bryant, my grandmother, had made the trip with us, and even though she was elderly at the time, she was a source of comfort for Betty. Lula May didn't drive on the trip, but she helped with Betsy and me and rubbed my mother's neck during the long drive home, which seemed longer returning than it did going. Little did we anticipate what was going to develop in the war or the dangerous path our patriarch would have to walk. I remember many fervent prayers lifted to the Almighty for those fighting on the battlefront and for our nation during those years. Unlike today, everyone invoked God's blessing on our country and the fighting soldiers. The freedom to mention God or pray was not diminished in any conversation, public or private.

With the realization that the Alaskan Campaign was over for my father, the grim reality began to sink in that, most likely, his next assignment was Europe. All of us realized that, wherever my father's assignment was, it would be more dangerous than Alaska. Thus, our prayers became more regular and fervent. It made us long for the day when he would come home for good and for lasting peace.

By this time, Betty had become an effective manager of the farm. Even though she was not raised in a rural environment, she worked hard and did the best she could to run the farm. She planted and harvested crops, managed the sharecroppers, made a garden, made molasses, and cut and marketed logs from the farm. She tried to cut timber in the Winter to take advantage of the idle labor after harvest. She also employed men to clear land and sell the logs. During the war, timber sold at excellent prices. Each sharecropper family had a team of mules, and they were used in the timber cutting and handling. Of course, each man thought his team was the best and would bet and brag as to how much they could pull.

On one occasion, I remember we left the woods with three wagons loaded down with logs. The first wagon made it through a bad mud hole, but the second got stuck. Albert Battle was the driver of the stuck wagon and was embarrassed because he had really bragged on his team, ole Dick and Dave. Albert proceeded to whip his team unmercifully and called them every name in the book. Ole Dick and Dave balked like some mules do when they get hurt, and when they do balk, they will not move. In desperation, Albert took some hay from the third wagon, spread it under Dick and Dave, and lit it with a match. The fire caused Dick and Dave to stomp and kick, and then they pulled up just enough to catch the wagon and axle grease on fire. The wagon was destroyed along with some logs; I guess Dick and Dave had the last laugh. After that, Albert never bragged on his team again.

Mules were very important in those days before we had tractors. A fond image in my mind of that bygone era was seeing the teams coming in from the fields at quitting time. After plowing all day, each man would come to the barn riding one mule and leading the other. Many times they would be singing, glad the hot day was over. I would race down the road in order to ride the mule that was being led back to the barn and then race back to catch another. Oh, how I wish I could see and hear those scenes again, and I treasure those memories of people and times forever gone.

Everyone had a "mule story" that we would enjoy from time to time. One sharecropper, Will Bill Battle, said, "A mule will work for you faithfully all his life just to get to kick you once real good." Nostalgic as mules were, we were all glad when John Deere and Allis Chalmers tractors came on the scene.

After enduring family separation, rations and uncertainty, we had no idea that the worst part of the war was still yet to come. In any event, we were most happy and thankful to have had this two-week visit with our family patriarch. The farm was intact, and we all hoped and prayed for better times for our nation in the future. Meanwhile, Carl Jones was being ordered to make a change of venue, and would soon be fighting Hitler in the European Theater.

Mule Barn About 1945

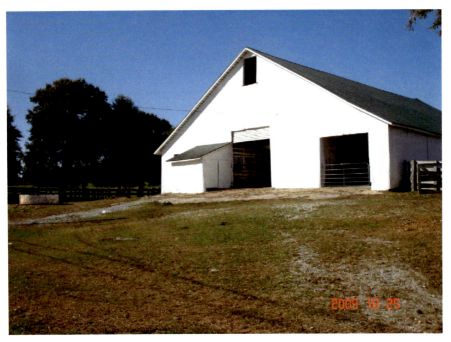

Mule Barn Today

Chapter 14 - Warminster

The Army Air Force DC-3 arrived in Washington D.C. on time and picked up Colonel Carl T. Jones along with several other officers and was airborne by 5:30 a.m. When the old DC-3 "Gooney Bird" was aloft, Carl made his way to the cockpit and asked the pilot where the group was going. The pilot replied, "Sir, I can't tell you until after our refueling stop in Newfoundland". The DC-3 is slow but very reliable, and after refueling, the pilot told the group that their destination was London, England. With this, the group settled back for several hours as the flight proceeded over the North Atlantic en route to their new assignments. None of them knew just where they would be assigned to fight Hitler and his henchmen. As the hours and miles rolled by, however, they realized they were nearing the thick of the fight in this war and that their future was uncertain.

The flight and landing was smooth, and several vehicles awaited the passengers as they deplaned. One Army private found my dad, asked if he was Colonel Carl T. Jones, and invited him into an Army sedan. The driver informed Carl that he was to take him and his gear to Boyton Manor in Warminster, England, which was about a two hour drive. Having never been to England, Carl was impressed by the sprawling English estates with their well-kept grounds and gardens.

Upon arrival at Boyton Manor House, he noticed how similar it was to other estates. The home was a two-story building with extra rooms in the attic dormers. Several Army vehicles were parked outside, and Carl was invited to report to the office of the XIX Corps commanding officer. Carl had no idea who he was reporting to as he waited at the reception desk outside the XIX Corps commanding general's office. When he did get the call to enter, he was greatly surprised to see Major General Charles Corlett, his old commanding officer in Alaska. After a warm salute, handshake, and greeting, General Corlett asked Carl to take a seat in his office. In the next few minutes, General Corlett told Carl of the plan to land forces in Normandy, France. He went on to tell Carl that he was the only living engineer officer in the U.S. Army who had planned a successful amphibious landing. In fact, he had helped plan two amphibious landings: Attu and Kiska. For the next hour, Corlett outlined the top secret plan of a future Normandy invasion to Carl.

    Carl had been personally recruited by Corlett, who was now commander of the XIX Corps. The operations order for the Omaha Beach portion of the Normandy invasion was to be planned in the Boyton Manor House by Carl and about fifty other personnel. Most of the other officers involved with writing this operations order were West Point graduates. Carl quickly pointed out to the General that West Pointers are usually not very fond of National Guardsmen. Corlett said he was well aware of that fact and would insist on everyone working together. He went on to express his confidence in Carl and the fact that considerable engineering expertise was needed for the landing in Normandy. The landing must have complete secrecy, and everyone in Boyton Manor would be locked in until the landing effort was consummated. Corlett said, "Carl, from this moment on, the only way anyone will leave Boyton is death. If you get sick, we will treat you. You will eat, sleep, and live in these quarters until the troops are ashore."

General Corlett was true to his word and instructed his men not to impose their feelings or rank on any member of the team, but to work together as one. He went on to stress that, for the invasion to be successful, all details had to be near perfect, and that cooperation and harmony had to exist as the plans were prepared. Many lives depended on the quality of their plan.

The operations order team was to work as many hours as they could, which finally amounted to 18-20 hours each day. They were fed as needed, and nearby cots provided a limited amount of sleep. Carl later said that, as the days progressed and the team got to know and appreciate each other, their planning and progress on the order improved. None of the team sequestered in the manor house were allowed any outside contact. Even mail contact was suspended and every avenue of secrecy was exercised.

The operations order effort lasted about sixty days. During that time, our family, as well as the other team member families, heard nothing from their soldiers. Unlike today, when we have almost instant communication, the soldiers in World War II had to depend almost entirely on the postal service. More often than not, when mail was received, the letter had been opened and censored by physically cutting out any words that might aid the enemy.

The operations order progressed slowly but deliberately. The first draft was very thick and laden with protective language for the career officers. Carl was able to convince the team to start over and make the order more concise and discernible to the foot soldier. The final draft was much smaller, and contained inserts that could be carried on the person of each company commander. Information on the beachhead and where everyone was could be very helpful to the engaged invasion units.

The main complaint against the final draft was that if the enemy were to get hold of that type of information, then a retreat of our forces could be compromised. Carl rose to his feet at the meeting stating that there was "no retreat from an amphibious landing. In an amphibious landing, you either win or get killed." At the time of the invasion of Normandy, the U.S. Army had almost zero experience in modern amphibious landings, save Attu and Kiska. The team forged ahead and the operations order was finally complete, even though some changes were still being made all the way up to the first part of June 1944.

While the operations order was being drafted, the Germans were busy bombing London almost nightly. Allied units were in preparation for the oncoming Normandy assault. British and American bomber and fighter planes were pounding German installations and towns with regularity. Some of the Allied Troops were seized with boredom having been in England for months awaiting an invasion. Carl stated that one of the most fearful attacks from the air was not the German bombers, but the V2 rocket.

The V1 rocket, sometimes called the "Buzz Bomb," could be heard and evasion could be implemented. The V2, however, was silent, and when you heard the explosion, it was too late. Fortunately, the Germans had not perfected an accurate guidance system at that time. The Allied Troops drilled, made ready their equipment, practiced on the rifle range, played cards, volleyball, and other games, and waited for the inevitable decision of when they would enter the war.

During this time, Carl met several men that later became household names in our home. One of these was a liaison officer from the British Army to the XIX Corps. His name was Major Vincent Weymouth, who they nicknamed "Hank the Yank." Hank and my dad became friends and even corresponded after the war. A Jeep driver by the name of Plott was assigned to drive my dad, and he stayed with him throughout the Normandy campaign and all the way into Germany.

During those 60 to 90 days of writing the Normandy operations order and waiting, my dad did not keep a detailed journal like he did in Alaska, probably because of the imperative for secrecy. This changed after he went ashore in France, as we will see later in this narrative. He did, however, start his European Campaign journal with pictures of Betty, Betsy, and me on page one with the emboldened words, "SOMETHING WORTH FIGHTING FOR."

The decision was finally made by General Dwight D. Eisenhower to launch the D-Day invasion of France on June 6, 1944. President Roosevelt subsequently asked the entire nation to get down on their knees and pray for the troops of the Allied Expeditionary Force. I remember well that this was done all over

America as Congress, churches, and individuals asked the Heavenly Father to protect our military men fighting Germany's madman and his NAZI tyranny over Europe.

My father's journal contains a copy of General Eisenhower's final communique to the soldiers, sailors, and airmen involved in the Allied Expeditionary Force on the eve of the D-Day invasion.

Boyton Manor in Warminster

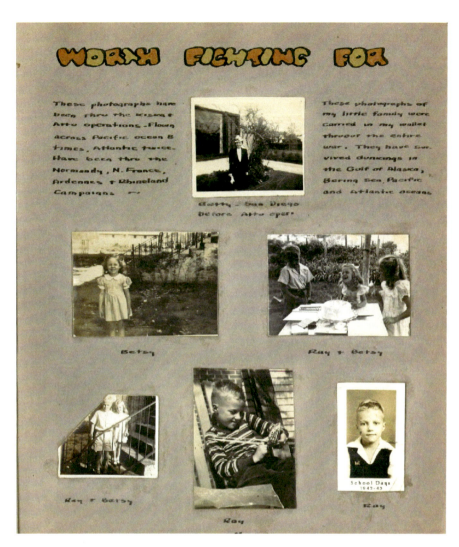

Worth Fighting For

Personal Notes

SUPREME HEADQUARTERS ALLIED EXPEDITIONARY FORCE

Soldiers, Sailors and Airmen of the Allied Expeditionary Force!

You are about to embark upon the Great Crusade, toward which we have striven these many months. The eyes of the world are upon you. The hopes and prayers of liberty-loving people everywhere march with you. In company with our brave Allies and brothers-in-arms on other Fronts, you will bring about the destruction of the German war machine, the elimination of Nazi tyranny over the oppressed peoples of Europe, and security for ourselves in a free world.

Your task will not be an easy one. Your enemy is well trained, well equipped and battle-hardened. He will fight savagely.

But this is the year 1944! Much has happened since the Nazi triumphs of 1940-41. The United Nations have inflicted upon the Germans great defeats, in open battle, man-to-man. Our air offensive has seriously reduced their strength in the air and their capacity to wage war on the ground. Our Home Fronts have given us an overwhelming superiority in weapons and munitions of war, and placed at our disposal great reserves of trained fighting men. The tide has turned! The free men of the world are marching together to Victory!

I have full confidence in your courage, devotion to duty and skill in battle. We will accept nothing less than full Victory!

Good Luck! And let us all beseech the blessing of Almighty God upon this great and noble undertaking.

Dwight D. Eisenhower

This was issued to us just prior to D-Day. It convinced any doubters that this was really it.

Copy of Communique From Eisenhower

Chapter 15 - Normandy

With planning for D-Day complete, the assault on northern France and its occupying Germans was launched on Tuesday, June 6, 1944 at 6:30 a.m. Numerous accounts of the invasion have been recorded, in written form and video documentaries. Most of these are extremely accurate and much more detailed than I will attempt to describe in this book. The entire invasion for the liberation of Europe was quite broad and extensive, involving 5,000 ships, 160,000 Allied troops, and stretched over a 50-mile front. The serious student of World War II can avail himself of a number of these documentaries. Several films have been produced about the D-Day invasion that are noteworthy: *Saving Private Ryan*, *The Longest Day*, and others detail much of what D-Day was like. In my opinion, two of the better books written about the invasion are: *D-Day June 6, 1944*, by Stephen Ambrose and *Omaha Beach*, by Stephen Zaloga.

My task in this book is to follow the footsteps of my father, Carl Jones, and his combat unit, the XIX Corps, as they were involved in this epic battle in Europe. Even though Carl was now an engineer officer in the XIX Corps, he was still under the command of his Alaskan commander, General Charles Corlett. In Alaska, he was in Corlett's "Long Knives" unit, and in the XIX Corps he was in Corlett's "Tomahawks" unit. Corlett used Carl as his troubleshooter, often sending him forward to check on the conditions of roads and bridges as the XIX Corps moved across Europe.

Corlett and his staff crossed the English Channel and went ashore in France on D+4 (June 10). The invasion plan for Normandy designated five assault beach landings: Omaha, Utah, Gold, Juno, and Sword. These landings would become the largest amphibious landings in the history of warfare. The entire landing went under the code name of "Operation Neptune."

Omaha Beach was the most heavily defended by the Germans. Taking the beach was the responsibility of the units of the XIX Corps. The lead unit was the 29th infantry division alongside the 1st Army infantry division. American casualties on Omaha Beach were 5,000 men, dying mostly in the first few hours of the assault. The 29th and 1st had a combined force of 34,250 soldiers. Gradually these men were able to establish a beachhead after much bitter fighting. Fortunately, the attack surprised the Germans because of bad weather on June 5th. Most of their leadership took the day off and relaxed their guard. Hitler also overslept, and his officers were reluctant to wake him, thus allowing Allied troops valuable time to move inland from the beach. Had Hitler given the order to move two reserve panzer divisions into the fray, then the outcome of the D-Day invasion could have been significantly different.

As my father crossed Omaha Beach following the advancing army moving inland, he noticed some of the horrors of war: fallen soldiers, damaged equipment and vehicles, as well as a large number of abandoned rifles. There were stacks of .30 caliber carbine rifles on the beach. Evidently, our attacking soldiers abandoned these carbines and secured for themselves the more reliable M1 rifles.

The XIX Corps established its headquarters at noon on June 14th and took command of the central sector of the American front on the Cherbourg Peninsula. A major objective for the landing in Normandy was to invade German forces occupying Cherbourg. The XIX Corps consisted of artillery, armored, engineer, and reconnaissance units, as well as the 29th and the 30th infantry divisions.

The advance south from Omaha Beach toward their first objective, the French town of St. Lo, was begun immediately. Unfortunately, this was hedgerow country with sunken roads that afforded the Germans excellent concealment. The push toward St. Lo was slow because of those conditions, and the fact that the German soldiers were good fighters and gave ground only reluctantly.

My father said that the German soldier was, as an individual, exemplary. They were well equipped, disciplined, and dedicated, but they seemed to know nothing about teamwork. U.S. boys grew up playing on ball teams and seemed to be better fighters because they fought as a team, which won many battles for our side.

Once during these hedgerow battles, General Corlett sent Carl forward to rate the capacity of a bridge in the XIX Corps' path. Carl and his Jeep driver Plott, sped toward the bridge, but were attacked and strafed by a German Messerschmidt fighter plane. Immediately, Carl and Plott dove into one of the sunken hedgerow roads. Carl peered out into a field next to the hedgerow and saw two German cavalrymen galloping their horses across the field. Also, at the same time, our Allied troops nearby were shooting at the Germans and killed both of them and their horses. One of the horses fell on my dad, who was still in the sunken road. Carl and Plott were being strafed by a German fighter plane while at the same time Americans were shooting at the German cavalrymen. While all this was going on, Carl retrieved his pocket knife and cut the saddle girt from the dead horse. When the shooting stopped, Carl retrieved both saddles and the helmets from the dead Germans. Somehow he got home with these items, and I still have the saddles and one of the helmets. Carl and Plott were not hurt, but their Jeep was damaged pretty badly, so the bridge rating had to wait until the next day.

Just prior to engaging St. Lo, the XIX Corps was ordered to transfer command of the 30th Infantry Division to the VII Corps, and in return, picked up the 35th Infantry Division. Together, these two divisions attacked St. Lo. After a week of bitter hedgerow fighting, St. Lo fell on the 18th of July. A few days later, Carl was sent to determine the best route for the advancing Allied Army. (See photograph of St. Lo at the end of this chapter.) St. Lo was totally destroyed and, altogether, the XIX Corps lost 10,000 men taking the town and its surrounding area.

In the path of the XIX Corps lay the French towns of Canisy, Villebouden, and St. Manvieu Botage, which offered similar resistance, but not as severe as the hedgerow country around St. Lo. The town of Vire was reached on August 12. By this time, General Omar Bradley had assumed overall command of this sector of the fighting in France. My dad was very fond of General Bradley, describing him as a real leader who related well with his men. Carl and Omar Bradley stayed in contact with each other after the war. As a young man, I remember his visit to see our farm in Jones Valley and watching this famous general jump out of the truck to open the gates as we rode around the farm.

The XIX Corps slugged it out with the German Army across Northern France. Even though progress was slow, they seized the French towns Martain, Demfront, Alencon, and others, and crossed the Seine River on September 1st and crossed the Somme River on September 2nd. The XIX Corps and its units had to pay a price for traveling too fast and outrunning its supply lines. By this time, the German Army was retreating as fast as it could to prevent encirclement by Allied Forces. The XIX Corps had made a remarkable advance, and on September 2nd, their advance units crossed into the Belgian City of Tournai. The XIX Corps had to wait in Tournai until gas and supply lines caught up with them. The Germans used this time to regroup, blow up bridges, and prepare defensive fortifications. Most of these river crossings were pontoon boat bridges built by engineers of the XIX Corps. (See picture at the end of this chapter.)

When the XIX Corps reached the Albert Canal, General Corlett sent Carl forward to locate a site suitable for crossing with a pontoon boat bridge. To Carl's surprise, the bridge he was to consider replacing was still intact and in pretty good shape. Carl also had orders to look for an armored unit with which headquarters had lost contact. Since the bridge was intact, Carl continued several miles farther into enemy territory in search of the lost armored unit.

After several miles, he found them. The commander saluted Carl and verified that his was the lost armored unit. Then he said, "Colonel, do you realize that you are behind enemy lines and we are surrounded by Germans? I'm virtually out of gas and my men and equipment are pretty badly shot up. I've decided to move to the back of the wooded cove over to our right and try to survive until the army catches up with us. I have quite a number of wounded men, and most of the fight in my unit is weak at present."

Carl concurred with his decision because he knew an armored unit without gas is helpless. The commander invited Carl and Plott to stay with them since they were all behind enemy lines. Carl decided to stay with the armored unit, and he and Plott camped out in an army weapons carrier borrowed from the trapped unit.

For two long weeks they lay camouflaged in their cove retreat watching German convoys move back and forth across the front of the cove. Carl knew that the road they were using led to the intact bridge. Obviously, the Germans were using the bridge both ways, but mainly to retreat. About this time, General George Patton made his famous "end run" across France, which dealt a devastating blow to the German Army. Carl and his newly acquired armored unit friends heard the Patton radio talk and could tell that things were not going well for the German Army, which now was in full retreat. They decided to use what strength they had left to plug the east side of the bridge and trap the remaining Germans on the west side. This maneuver was skillfully done by the armored unit commander, and literally thousands of German soldiers were captured. Carl returned and reported to General Corlett, who was greatly relieved to see him, as he was on the verge of filing a Missing in Action report on him.

In early September, the XIX Corps had advanced well into Northern France toward Belgium and had been engaged militarily in dozens of French towns. Carl recalled the fact that the French people in these towns greeted our soldiers as heroes. For the most part, they were excited to be freed from NAZI rule. The only hostile French group they encountered was the "Free French." Carl said that the "Free French" would shoot at either side, German or our Allied troops. The Germans fought using delaying tactics and gave up ground reluctantly. Each town had its own value to the German empire, and Allied Troops paid dearly for every French and Belgium village. Somehow the perseverance and resolve to win this war never left the American and Allied soldiers. It seems the soldiers fighting in World War II exhibited more fortitude to win and to retaliate for the evil done by the Axis powers than by most any military force in history.

Carl T. Jones

German Cavalry Saddle and Helmet

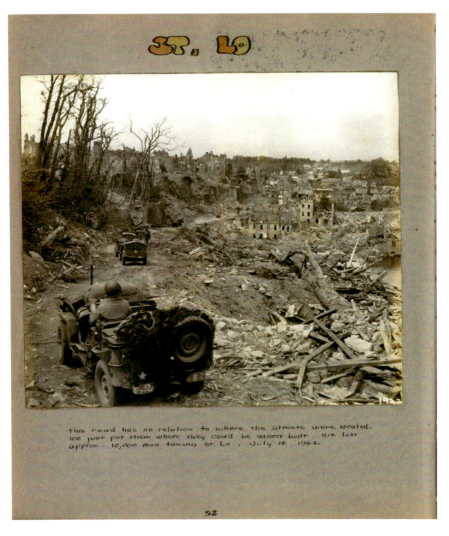

This road has no relation to where the streets were located. We just put them where they could be easiest built. We lost approx. 10,000 men taking St. Lo, July 16, 1944.

St. Lo

Seine River Crossing

Chapter 16 - Belgium / Holland

The XIX Corps reached the Seine River on August 28, 1944, and crossed on September 1st. The XIX Corps had fought across Northern France and in numerous villages along the way. One month before crossing the Seine River, they had been fighting on the outskirts of Paris. Their course of fighting the stubborn German Army had taken them in a northerly direction toward the Seine and the country of Belgium.

Carl noted that the crush of the battle left the French landscape in devastation with death everywhere along the way. Cattle, horses, and human remains were littered along each road. The German Army had lost over 100,000 soldiers in the Falaise-Argentan area, mostly by capture. Carl noted that the retreating German Army had mined everything they could in an effort to inflict as much possible harm to the pursuing Allied soldiers. One of the tasks assigned to a combat engineer unit is to clear the area of mines. Carl noted that many a good American soldier was killed or maimed for life while clearing these German mine fields.

On September 2nd, at 0930, the first Allied troops entered Belgium. Later that day, the first large Belgium city, Tournai, fell to the XIX Corps; and by midnight, three-fourths of the corps was on Belgian soil. The countryside and people of Belgium were very similar to those in Northern France. The XIX Corps route took them south of the rather large city of Brussels.

The command of the XIX Corps was surprised at how quickly the country of Belgium fell. Belgium was not as large an area as Northern France, and by that time the German Army had expended a lot of its energy and had lost some of its dedication. It took just ten days to cross the country, and on September 12th, they reached and crossed the Meuse River into the Maastrict area of Holland. By then, the German Army had blown all the bridges crossing the river and its surrounding canals, so combat engineers were kept busy building replacement crossings.

Pontoon and Bailey bridges were the most often used, and each bridge site had to be selected, planned, and designed by combat engineers. Carl was called on for many of these bridge site crossings and had several close calls while dodging enemy fire. Interestingly, soldiers of the XIX Corps were the first Allied troops to enter Belgium, as well as Holland. The next day, September 13th, Maastrict fell. And four days later, Heerlen, Holland fell after bitter fighting along a well-prepared line of German defense. With Heerlen in hand, the XIX Corps was only two days from the supposedly impenetrable Siegfried Line. It was here in Heerlen that Carl had a unique experience that would influence him and his family for the rest of their lives.

LOUT

By mid-October, there was a change of command for the XIX Corps. Lt. General Raymond S. McLain had replaced General Charles Corlett, who was needed elsewhere in the European Theater. General McLain decided to keep Carl serving as an engineering troubleshooter. McLain assigned Carl the task of going to Heerlen and establishing contact with the Dutch Underground there. Carl proceeded to Heerlen early the next morning, armed with limited information about the location of the Dutch Underground's headquarters. After several false visits to suspected contact locations, Carl was finally directed to the basement of a fairly intact building.

Upon entering the busy basement office, he identified himself to a receptionist and asked to meet with the leader of their Dutch resistance organization. In broken English, the receptionist asked him to wait. In a few minutes, a rather pretty young lady showed up and, in better English, asked if he was Colonel Carl T. Jones of the XIX Corps. Carl replied that he was, but that he "would really like to meet with the leader of the Heerlen Dutch resistance organization." She replied, "My name is Lout Ottenhoff, and I am the leader of the Dutch Resistance here." Carl was very surprised that this young woman was his contact.

Over the next few days, she shared several things with Carl about the strategic advantages of the area and slowly they became friends. She shared with him how delighted the people of the Netherlands were that America and the other Allied troops were fighting the Germans. The German Army had occupied the Netherlands for a long time and had inflicted many atrocities against the Dutch people. The Germans had plundered and destroyed most of the buildings and meaningful monuments of the country. She reported that most of the country's historical treasures and art had been hidden in caves, and that the Germans had not found them. The main purpose of her organization was to make things as difficult for the occupying German Army as possible. Lout's father was a medical doctor, and one of their objectives was to find, treat, hide, and deport Allied airmen that had been shot down, so they could fly again.

One day, Lout invited my father to dinner at her family home. Carl met the Ottenhoff family and had dinner with them several times while he was in Heerlen. (A picture of the Ottenhoff family is at the end of this chapter.) Carl noticed that even though Mrs. Ottenhoff's food was good, it was meager, and it bothered him later that he had eaten some of their short food supply. The next day, he loaded up all the food from one of the mess halls that his Jeep could carry and replenished the Ottenhoff family with some much needed food supply. The family was so very grateful for this gift because they had suffered and lived with shortages for a long time.

Later, he found out, that for most of the last year of the war, the Dutch people had eaten mostly tulip bulbs. Their country had been made desolate by the German occupation, thus further explaining their elation at finally being liberated.

Years later, Lout came to my hometown and confided in me that she had never been able to forgive the Germans for what they did to her country. She said, with tears in her eyes, that she had prayed about it and had diligently sought to forgive them, but she couldn't. She said that one of the favorite actions of the occupying Germans was to go to a Dutch home and take the youngest child out in the yard and shoot the child while the family watched.

Lout made several visits to my hometown of Huntsville, Alabama in the years after the war, and we all became close to this brave woman who had befriended my dad. Lout also looked after the grave of my cousin, Nelson Jones, who was killed in Germany and is buried near Heerlen in America's Margraten National Cemetery. Lout put little yellow flowers on Nelson's grave for as long as her health would allow. Lout is dead now, but her memory lives on in our family.

The following is a letter I wrote to the Jones family on May 19, 1998 as my wife Libby and I returned from visiting Lout and her husband Htenk Callis, as well as Nelson's grave in Holland.

>May 19, 1998
>Members of Nelson Jones' Family:
>Recently, Libby and I made a trip to Europe and included a trip to Holland for the purpose of visiting Nelson's grave.
>On Saturday the 16th of May we arrived in Amsterdam a little before noon. A driver had been pre-arranged to meet us, and after retrieving our bags, we started toward the cemetery near Margraten Holland via of a village called Vaals in order to meet Htenk and Lout Callis. The trip took about 2 ½ hours along an excellent road and some beautiful countryside which was mostly dairy cattle, sheep, and some vegetable farming. The traffic was bad at times, but our driver, Rene, was a good one and we had no trouble finding the old hotel at Vaals and Htenk and Lout Ottenhoff. We had lunch there at the hotel, showed pictures of Aunt Hazel, Carl and Betty and our children and grandchildren and just visited for quite a long time about the war, as well as experiences of our relationship over the years. We rode with Htenk and Lout to the cemetery with our driver following, during which

they both related stories about the war. Htenk was 19 when the war ended; surviving the last year of the war by eating tulip bulbs. Lout talked about meeting Carl and about her family's involvement in the Dutch Underground. She said that on Carl's first visit to dinner at their home he felt he had eaten too much of the meal Mrs. Ottenhoff had prepared and apologized profusely. The next day, a Jeep showed up with enough food to last the family for two weeks. Their stories are so vivid and terrible about the war and its suffering. Episodes of a horrible time in history that I'm afraid has been mostly forgotten by the younger generation of Holland, as well as our own nation.

Upon arriving at the cemetery, one is immediately impressed with the well-kept, immaculate grounds that comprise the plot of ground on which our brave soldiers are buried. Rhododendrons, flowers, roses, and perfectly cut grass surround acres of little white crosses all perfectly aligned no matter which direction one may look. Each cross bears the soldier's name and rank, military unit, and the state from whence the soldier came. Nelson's grave is near the front entrance on the right-hand side. Lout had brought some yellow flowers that she placed at the base of Nelson's stone cross, which she has done many times over the years.

I cannot adequately express how I felt standing next to Nelson's grave. Nelson was my childhood hero. When Nelson left to go to war, I was about nine years old, and he was a recently graduated high school senior, as well as president of the senior class. To a nine-year-old, I suppose a high school senior is about as important as they come. If there ever was an "all American" fine, young man that put on a uniform and marched into war, it was Nelson. Somehow, though, he had a premonition about what was to happen, because the Christmas before he left, he stated that this would be his last with the family. The following April 2, 1945, he made the supreme sacrifice for our nation. Each little white cross represents a life that was given toward our country's effort in the war, all with the same accord as Nelson's, which was to stop the madman in Berlin and the atrocities he inflicted on millions of families all over the world.

We took pictures of Nelson's grave and the cemetery, some of which I've enclosed, in addition to some including Htenk and Lout. They are getting on in age and have been wonderful friends over the years. They have visited Nelson's grave many times with members of our family who have traveled to Holland. Walter and Hazel, Betty and Carl, Doug and Bonnie, and others that I may not know about have been recipients of Htenk and Lout Callis' hospitality and love for a man named Nelson that they never met. War does many terrible things to a family, none the least of which is losing one of its members. Aren't we fortunate to have been blessed with this couple from Holland named Callis that befriended our family and placed flowers on Nelson's grave for these many years?

A tall building in the center of the cemetery serves as a chapel with a set of chimes. It is flanked by two long walls bearing the names of those soldiers whose resting place is known only to God. On the hour, the chimes play "America" both day and night. A wall near the front displays the Battle for Europe and the various units as they proceeded against the Germans. The entire plot of ground leaves one feeling proud to be an American and knowing that our fallen soldiers are being well cared for. Incidentally, Carl Jones was given the task of selecting this cemetery site as one of his Engineer Officer duties. Little did he know that it would become the resting place for one of our family members and receive visits from the family many years later.

We said goodbye to Htenk and Lout for several long minutes, each hoping that they could visit each other soon. Two and a half hours later, we were in Amsterdam at our hotel where we said goodbye to our excellent driver, Rene. Libby and I were tired but most thankful for having made this trek to Nelson's grave. This I have wanted to do for over three decades. Somehow I wanted to stand in the place where my "childhood" hero was buried and express a silent appreciation to him and the other brave men there for the measure of freedom we enjoy today. I pray that our nation and its future generations will not forget the sacrifice made by so many during this terrible war. It would be inconceivable to think that this plot of ground in Margraten Holland was the resting place of men who died in vain.

I suppose the inscription on the chapel tower says it best:

"In memory of the valor and the sacrifices which hallow this soil."

Affectionately,
Ray Jones

Ottenhoff Family

Nelson's Grave

Chapter 17 - Germany

Southern Holland is very close to Germany and the next objective of the XIX Corps was the city of Aachen, Germany. In the 1930s, the Germans constructed the Siegfried Line as a permanent military protection for their country. This line built along the German border consisted of a series of reinforced concrete pyramid-shaped obstacles, usually four deep, designed to stop or impede an invading army. The Germans called this obstacle "the west wall" and they felt safe thinking the Siegfried line would forever protect their Deutschland. General Patton reportedly said that "any army's fixed fortifications are a monument to the stupidity of man."

The German Army's resistance stiffened considerably, as they now fought on their own soil. Counter attacks became more common, and the fighting in the villages was house to house. In spite of this, the XIX Corps launched a powerful offensive on October 2, 1944 and breached the Siegfried Line in its path. A hole in the line eleven miles wide and four miles deep was opened by Corps engineers using heavy equipment and explosives, and the XIX Corps encircled and cut off the last escape route from Aachen.

Aachen fell on October 16th after much bitter fighting. American forces were elated as they pushed east of the Wurm River.

Carl was one of the first officers to arrive in Aachen after it fell. A large NAZI flag was still flying over the captured enemy headquarters when Carl reached that location. One of the soldiers asked Carl what should be done with the NAZI flag. Carl said he didn't know and instructed the soldier to just stuff it in his duffel bag and he would deal with it later. Somehow, Carl made it home with that flag, and I still have it in my home. (See photograph of this flag at the end of this chapter.) The flag is a very large cotton red flag (9 x16 ½ ft.) with a black swastika in its middle. The hand-stitching on the flag was most likely done by some German women or by some of the Jewish slave labor in German camps. The flag is in excellent shape and is a permanent reminder to all that see it of this terrible war.

Having smashed the Siegfried Line and captured Aachen, the XIX Corps pushed northeast to the Roer River, thus setting the stage for a final drive into the heart of Germany. General Eisenhower announced that there would be no Winter lull in the pursuit of the enemy. The fighting was as intense as any encountered since the landing in Normandy.

On the 16th of November, elements of the XIX Corps drove across the flat, battle-scarred, muddy countryside of Germany against stubborn German resistance. The Germans committed its two best panzer divisions in an effort to halt the XIX Corps. The German resistance effort failed and many enemy tanks and soldiers fell before the offensive attack. Captured German staff officers were unanimous in their praise of the tactics employed by the XIX Corps offensive drive. The officers commented that they were constantly confused as to the direction and strength of the Allied forces opposing them.

Planning for the drive across the Roer River was well underway when the German counter offensive in the Ardennes forced a postponement. This counter offensive eventually became known as the "Battle of the Bulge." For the first time since the landing in Normandy, the XIX Corps had to change from an offensive effort to a defensive one. In the bitter cold of Winter, the Corps held the north shoulder of the "Bulge" and undertook local attacks to keep the German forces busy.

Carl and the Corps headquarters personnel hunkered down and spent a cheerless Christmas in an old monastery at Kornelimunster. Most of the fighting was to the south of their position, around Marche and Bastogne. Hitler again miscalculated the resilience of the American soldier, even when fighting in the snow and a bitter cold winter. Allied losses were heavy, and the suffering from the weather was almost unbearable. Carl said that one of his most emotional memories of that Christmas was one night when he walked up on a group of GIs, huddled around a fire trying to keep warm and they were singing "Silent Night." Obviously, their thoughts were of a home and a far away land called America.

It was during this time that General McLain sent for Carl. Upon reporting, McLain directed that Carl return to Southern Holland and find at least three sites for a possible national cemetery in which to bury our dead. "Do not pick a site in Germany," McLain instructed. "We will not bury American soldiers on German soil," the General went on to say.

Carl left that same day and retraced his steps to the Maastrict area of Holland. Carl's first contact was Lout. And after explaining that his mission was to identify a cemetery site, she indicated that she knew of a farm that would be perfect. In the next few days, they identified three potential sites with the preference to the beautiful farm Lout had first mentioned, which encompassed 65 ½ acres. This site was eventually chosen, and the first American soldiers that fell in Germany were buried in this cemetery named Margraten. Margraten, one of America's national cemeteries, is located halfway between Maastricht and Aachen, and the cemetery is beautiful. There are 8,301 of our soldiers buried in Margraten, which is one of nine such cemeteries in Europe, and it is the third most populated. France has five cemeteries. Belgium has two. Luxembourg and Holland have one each. These cemeteries are America's last way to honor these dead heroes, young men who, by all rights, should have been at home working and raising a family. Instead, they were called to arms to fight in a foreign land all because of an ungodly, overbearing leader who committed unspeakable acts of aggression upon innocent people.

Above the cemetery's Chapel, these words are engraved:

"IN MEMORY OF THE VALOR
AND THE SACRIFICES WHICH
HALLOW THIS SOIL."

Finally, on the 5th of February, the XIX Corps moved north again toward the Roer River. The Germans were in full retreat by this time, and they used one of their last delaying tactics by blowing a dam on the Roer River to flood the pursuing Allied Forces. The XIX Corps had no intention of waiting until the river subsided; they waited only until the speed of the current had diminished enough to be bridged.

The crossing of the Roer River was probably one of the most difficult river crossings in military history. The XIX Corps Engineers built 15 bridges across the flooded river. One of them was rebuilt nine times. Across the Roer, there was no pause in the attack. The Germans expended their last serious attack of the war in those bitter Winters of 1944 and 1945. As a nation, Germany had depleted most of its military forces, and the aggressive spirit of even Hitler was waning. The XIX Corps had its enemy on the run, and they allowed them no breathing space in which to stop and reorganize. The Corps stepped up its speed day by day, and the rush and retreat of the enemy never stopped, even when the Rhine River was reached. Unlike other river obstacles, the Germans didn't blow all the bridges on the Rhine. The rather large Remagen Bridge was a major crossing point, and it was left intact.

German soldiers were surrendering in mass during this time, as everyone on both sides sensed that the war would soon be over. Allied troops were speeding toward Berlin with the goal of taking over the German hierarchy. Allied spirits were high as victory seemed imminent. It was during this period of "close to victory" elation that the Allied command received some heartbreaking orders. All Allied commands were ordered to hold up just outside of Berlin and allow our Russian counterpart to take

East Berlin. Carl said that these orders were devastating to our troops who had fought so hard to liberate and conquer all of Europe, including Germany. Nevertheless, as history records, this is what happened, and Berlin became a source of conflict between the U.S. and Russia for the next four decades. Not until President Ronald Reagan persuaded Russian President Gorbachev on June 12, 1987 to "tear down this wall" did the Second World War completely end for Berlin.

For the most part, Carl and the XIX Corps had "clean up" duty and spent the next several weeks packing to return home. For them, the terrible war in Europe was essentially over. Their biggest challenge now was to find a way home as soon as possible.

Siegfried Line 1944

The Author with Nazi Flag taken from Aachen, Germany in 1944

Margraten Cemetery

Chapter 18 - Going Home

From the time the German defensive lines collapsed in late January of 1945, the end of the war in Europe was almost certain. Several world-changing events occurred in the first six months of 1945 that would greatly affect our family, as well as the nation. President Franklin D. Roosevelt passed away on April 1, 1945. Despite his infirmities of being confined to a wheelchair, he stood tall in the conflict. He led and forged a wonderful relationship with Sir Winston Churchill of England, a relationship that had a very effective influence on the war. Roosevelt was a natural and decisive leader of the country. His direction, along with many other leaders, both military and civilian, helped make an Allied victory possible. Years later, the journalist Tom Brokaw said that "those who waged war in World War II, both civilian and military, were the greatest generation," and no doubt they deserved this label. Vice President Harry Truman was the replacement of Roosevelt, and he too, was a staunch leader.

Thirty days after Roosevelt died, Hitler and his wife, Eva, committed suicide, which was the last World War II act of defiance by Germany. Within ten days, on May 7, 1945, Germany had surrendered. Allied forces formally declared May 8, 1945 as VE (Victory in Europe) Day. Most of the world, especially in Europe and the victorious Allied countries, celebrated the end of this part of World War II. Europe was mostly in shambles from the effects of the war. Whole cities in France, Belgium, Holland, and Germany were reduced to rubble. The surviving Europeans, nevertheless, celebrated along with the Allied victors. Hitler's Jewish death camps had been discovered and his heinous crimes against humanity exposed. In May of 1945, Europe was a scene of death, separation of families, and devastation of the countries that lay in the path of the opposing armies.

As one commentator opined, "It will take Europe many decades, if ever, to recover from this war's influence." The American loss in this European war was also great with 291,557 soldiers, sailors, and airmen killed, and 670,646 wounded. German losses in Europe were 3,250,000 combat troops killed and 7,250,000 wounded, and a civilian loss of over 1.6 million. What a price to pay for this godless madman dictator called Adolph Hitler, who wanted to conquer the world and eliminate the Jewish race.

On April 18, 1945, just 19 days before Germany surrendered, my first cousin, Nelson Jones, was killed in Oerlinghausen, Germany. Nelson paid the supreme price as a result of a shell bast from the big gun of a German panzer tank; so close to the war's end, yet so far. Nelson was in combat just 210 days after his enlistment with the 95th Infantry Division. He was president of his senior class in 1944 at Huntsville High School in Huntsville, Alabama, and was another example of a fine young man who was caught up in this terrible war. A war that inflicted a lot of pain and suffering on the families of all the countries involved.

During this "stand-still period," Carl and the XIX Corps, were engaged with handling a glut of German prisoners and humanitarian issues involving the beaten German population. Carl noted that the displaced and orphaned children tugged at the heartstrings of soldiers more than anything else.

In mid-May, Carl was offered a promotion to the rank of Brigadier General if he would stay and help with the rebuilding of parts of Europe destroyed in the war. Carl didn't hesitate in turning down the offer, stating that he was appreciative, but had a family and a farm at home that he had scarcely seen in five years. The next week he received orders to return to Washington for a post war debriefing inquisition, as soon as practical.

In mid-June, he began his trip back to the Washington debriefing, having to "hitchhike" on planes headed west. Before leaving, he said goodbye to his faithful Jeep driver Plott, as well as the headquarters personnel with whom he had served for most of the past year. One of the legs of his flight home landed at Maastricht, Holland, and he was able to say goodbye to the Ottenhoff family and visit Nelson's grave.

It took about twelve days, layovers included, to finally touch down in Washington and this blessed land called America. Upon landing, Carl, along with every soldier on the plane knelt down and kissed the ground and thanked the Lord that they had once again returned to our homeland. With the exception of fighting Japan in the South Pacific, the war was mostly over for our country.

The debriefing, Carl learned, would last several weeks and would be held entirely at the Pentagon in Washington, D.C. Carl called Betty and asked her to bring Betsy and me to Washington as soon as possible. So, once again, we loaded up the 1939 Pontiac and went back to Washington to see our patriarch. Washington was alive with military personnel returning home from the European Theater. Everyone was in a bright mood as they anticipated complete victory over Japan to finally end World War II.

The first atomic bomb was dropped on Hiroshima on August 6, 1945, and three days later a second bomb was dropped on Nagasaki, Japan. The result was devastating to these two cities. Even though Japan started the conflict by bombing Pearl Harbor, and most likely expected some retaliation, they had had enough. On August 15, 1945, our nation declared VJ (Victory over Japan) Day to be the war's end. On September 2, 1945, Japan signed an unconditional surrender treaty, thus officially ending this terrible war.

On the night of VJ Day, our family was in Washington, D.C., visiting my father. Neither video nor smart phone equipment was available in those days, but I have wished many times that we could have recorded the scenes in Washington that night.

Even though we had an automobile, the vehicle was useless because of the throngs of people everywhere. Carl insisted that this was a significant event in our country's history, and that we should walk to 1600 Pennsylvania Avenue, the White House, and view as well as relish the occasion with the jubilant crowd. We walked for a long time while passing laughing, singing, and joyful people. Policemen would stop directing traffic to kiss a pretty girl. Many soldiers stopped to hug my mother or to high-five me or toss Betsy into the air. My father was in full uniform with his

Colonel's Eagle showing, but was still bear-hugged by several enlisted men. President Truman came out on the White House porch and waved to the crowd. Bands played and people danced at almost every intersection. I'm sure that military victors have celebrated when returning from battle over the centuries, but few could rival this one that night in Washington, D.C. We didn't get back to our apartment until about 3 a.m. the next morning, but no one cared. Betsy went to sleep on our return journey, and we took turns carrying her. The celebration lasted well into the next day and night, but with less spontaneous energy. We stayed for a few more days before leaving for home. We visited the Washington museums again and paddled boats on the Tidal Basin while enjoying being with my father once again.

The trip home was uneventful, except for signs of victory in every town and hamlet. This country and its people were elated to finally be free from the bondage of war.

Millions of prayers had been lifted up to God for our country and its fighting men. Most of those prayers had been answered and the war was finally over. Of all the prayers entreated by America for those fighting in Europe, I suppose that the prayer of our President, Franklin D. Roosevelt, was one of the most heartfelt.

PRAYER OF PRESIDENT FRANKLIN D. ROOSEVELT DELIVERED ON A NATIONAL RADIO BROADCAST ON THE EVENING OF JUNE 6, 1944 – D-DAY IN NORMANDY, FRANCE:

President Franklin D. Roosevelt read this prayer on a national radio broadcast on the evening of June 6, 1944 – D-Day, the day on which Allied troops stormed the beaches of Normandy.

>Almighty God:
>
>Our sons, pride of our nation, this day have set upon a mighty endeavor, a struggle to preserve our republic, our religion, and our civilization, and to set free a suffering humanity.
>
>Lead them straight and true; give strength to their arms, stoutness to their hearts, steadfastness in their faith.
>
>They will need Thy blessings. Their road will be long and hard. For the enemy is strong. He may hurl back our forces. Success may not come with rushing speed, but we shall return again and again; and we know that by Thy grace, and by the righteousness of our cause, our sons will triumph.
>
>They will be sore tired, by night and by day, without rest, until the victory is won. The darkness will be rent by noise and flame. Men's souls will be shaken with the violences of war.
>
>For these men are lately drawn from the ways of peace. They fight not for the lust of conquest. They fight to end conquest. They fight to liberate. They fight to let justice arise, and tolerance and good will among all Thy people. They yearn but for the end of battle, for their return to the haven of home.
>
>Some will never return. Embrace these, Father, and receive them, Thy heroic servants, into Thy Kingdom.
>
>And for us at home – fathers, mothers, children, wives, sisters, and brothers of brave men overseas –

whose thoughts and prayers are ever with them – help us, Almighty God, to rededicate ourselves in renewed faith in Thee in this hour of great sacrifice...

Let our hearts be stout, to wait out the long travail, to bear sorrows that may come, to impart our courage unto our sons wheresoever they may be.

And, O Lord, give us faith...Let not the keenness of our spirit ever be dulled. Let not the impacts of temporary events...deter us in our unconquerable purpose.

With Thy blessing, we shall prevail...Lead us to the saving of our country, and with our sister nations into a world unity that will spell a sure peace, a peace invulnerable to the schemings of unworthy men. And a peace that will let all of men live in freedom, reaping the just rewards of their honest toil.

Thy will be done, Almighty God. Amen.

VJ Day Photo

Credits: Eisenstaedt in Times Square, William C. Shrout—Time & Life Pictures/Getty Images

Part III

Chapter 19 - Starting Over

Life in America after the war was difficult. I suppose that could be said by every country that has experienced an extended war. An absence of leadership in every community for those four-plus war years had an impact on every city and state in the nation. Huntsville, Alabama was no exception. Madison County and its county seat of Huntsville was host to many families whose lives would never be the same because of this devastating war.

One significant memory I have of the returning soldiers was the emotional and loving expressions of their families when they saw them return. Recently, there have been several documentaries on T.V. showing these similar reactions when soldiers returned home from war. Sweethearts, wives, children, and friends were tearful and excited to see their returning hero. I have never forgotten these events in my life and still tear up when I see them today. Almost every family in America had such an event after World War II.

The returning of Huntsville's war veterans caused a change in the "pecking order" of the community's leadership. The soldiers returned with a spring in their step, somewhere between being thankful they were returning home alive, and looking forward to rebuilding their lives and their community.

G.W. Jones' three sons, one grandson, and one granddaughter returned home from the war, but fate would leave one grandson, Nelson, buried in southern Holland. Mothers across the nation were finally able to take down the stars hanging in their windows. "Mama" Jones (Mrs. G. W.) could finally take down the five blue stars and one gold star from her window on Randolph Street. All of the returning family of G.W. Jones threw themselves into trying to rebuild their lives, businesses, and professions. Walter resumed his post as Alabama's State Geologist. Howard Jr. returned to manage the Isaac Criner family farm on Mountain Fork Creek. Edith Jones (a Navy wave) became a medical doctor after the war. Edith married John Ledbetter, M.D., and they opened an office and the two of them served the town of Rogersville, Alabama for 48 years. Ed and Carl vigorously pursued improvements to the engineering firm and the farm in Jones Valley. To help with the task of rebuilding, several wonderful employees came into their business during this time, and most remained until their death.

Some of these were: Brigadier General J.O. Johnson who became the general manager of G.W. Jones and Sons (Huntsville's J.O. Johnson High School is named in his honor); Brigadier General Pat Patillo, an excellent engineer serving on General Patton's left flank during Patton's "end run" across Europe, who became a key engineer at G.W. Jones and Sons; U.G. Roberts, a former 1st Sergent in Alaska for Carl, who became the farm manager; Tom Johnson, J.O.'s brother, who became the "go to" man in the G.W. Jones and Sons office operations (the Huntsville

Madison County Jetplex Industrial Park was dedicated to the memory of Tom Johnson in 1990); Phoebe White, who managed and kept financial records for all the G.W. Jones entities for over 50 years; and Maureen Searcy, who came to work for the engineering department as a young bride and worked for the firm for over 50 years.

Luther Robinson became an employee favorite and worked for the firm for 68 years. At one time, G.W. Jones and Sons employed almost 100 persons. These, plus dozens more faithful and dedicated employees of G.W. Jones and Sons worked tirelessly for the firm and equally hard for the community. These employees, as well as many businessmen of Huntsville seemed to possess a sixth sense that "if it was good for the community, then it would eventually be good for all individually;" or, as President John F. Kennedy once put it: "A rising tide lifts all boats." At G.W. Jones and Sons, community advancement would take priority over most anything else, and this direction and attitude continued well into the 21st Century.

In the aftermath of World War II, Huntsville was struggling. Industry was nonexistent and the seven cotton textile mills that had existed in the 1930s and 40s had mostly closed down. Six of those mills were union organized, and only one (Huntsville Manufacturing Company) was not. The six union mills gradually closed their doors, whereas the Huntsville Manufacturing Company remained open until the late 1990s. The Huntsville leadership did not forget that event, and vowed to discourage an industry trying to locate in Madison County that brought with it a union workforce. For the most part, that influence still exists today. Huntsville is still known as a non-union town, whereas Florence, Gadsden, Birmingham, and others have struggled with their unionized industries.

Huntsville's leadership did everything it could to generate some business activity and commerce. The Chamber of Commerce worked hard to entice industry to locate in Huntsville, but to no avail. They formed the Huntsville Industrial Expansion Committee (HIEC), an offshoot of the Chamber, to specifically search for prospective industries. Carl Jones was selected to be Chairman of this committee and served in that capacity more than once. They made several trips to Washington, D.C. to lobby for projects and try to influence the Pentagon not to sell Redstone Arsenal.

Southern Railroad was looking for a route from Chicago to Mobile and the HIEC lobbied long and hard for that rail location only to see it go through Decatur. Still, another effort was to ask that a government proposed "wind tunnel" be built on Redstone Arsenal. That project was lost to Tullahoma, Tennessee.

The Chamber fostered and encouraged activity of every kind in the county. Street dances and cattle shows around the courthouse square were regular events. A lot of effort was expended in trying to find a use for Redstone Arsenal, which had been declared "army surplus" and was up for sale. Even though nothing seemed to work for those Huntsville servicemen returning from World War II, they still had a quiet confidence that things would change for the better. This was home, and they believed in this sleepy little cotton town that John Hunt homesteaded in 1805.

In 1950, the population of Huntsville was 16,437. Almost unknowingly, the city was on the verge of receiving a significant economic impact. During the Christmas season of 1949, Dr. Wernher von Braun and his team of German rocket scientists chose the Huntsville Arsenal as their desired location to build rockets for our country. They had been given the choice between six arsenals that had been declared surplus. It has been said that they chose Huntsville because it reminded them most of Bavaria in southern Germany. As a result of this decision, Huntsville and Madison County would never be the same.

At first, there was significant resistance by local citizens to the idea of having Germans as fellow citizens. I suppose this was understandable because, just a few years earlier, the Germans were killing many of our country's finest. Also during this period of time, there was resentment among some of Huntsville's citizens toward those who did not go to war. There were some able-bodied men that navigated a way out of the draft and military service. Naturally, the families whose loved ones were exposed to the horrors of war didn't have a high regard for those who they felt had shirked their duty.

I remember one such instance that happened to Carl after he returned home. Carl was in a 15-man meeting when he asked a question about why a project had gotten off on the wrong foot. One of the men blurted out, "Oh, you wouldn't know because you were off playing soldier at that time." There was an immediate silence in the room as Carl rose to his feet and looked straight in the man's eyes. After a few tense moments Carl said, "Sir, I spent five years of my life fighting for this country, and none of it was play. I fought for America and all of its people, including you, and I'm proud of my service. I am leaving this meeting, and I'll wait for you outside if you wish to settle this on the grass." With that he left and waited outside, but the man never showed up.

Gradually, feelings such as this, as well as the resentment toward the Germans, subsided. The German scientists subsequently became some of Huntsville's finest citizens, and they, too, fell in love with Huntsville and the area.

The reactivation of Redstone Arsenal provided Huntsville with an economic engine that has lasted over sixty years. The leadership of the city and county enthusiastically embraced the military and eventually the nation's space effort that would be entwined with Redstone Arsenal. Most of the local boards and civic positions were filled with these returning servicemen as the area began rebuilding our community.

One positive aspect that existed in America during the 1950s while the country was rebuilding was that possibly as many as 90% of American families were two-parent families. Sixty years later, according to recent statistics, a substantial number of children are reared in single-parent households! Obviously, the American family and its people have suffered a severe decline in values and dedication since those post World War II days.

If that same task of rebuilding was required by our country today, it would be most difficult because of the loss of those values held dear prior to World War II and the breakdown of the family.

Chapter 20 - Kentucky 31 Fescue

Carl and Ed returned their attention to the Jones Valley farm after the war. At that time it was a share-cropping cotton farm. Their absence during the war years had left the farm in a very difficult economic state. The principle crop during the 1940s in North Alabama had been cotton. Sharecroppers had farmed the land for decades. The boll weevil, johnsongrass, and other inhibitors of the crop made cotton very difficult to grow. There were no herbicides, pesticides, tractors, or mechanical machinery such as those that exist today to help the cotton farmer. Gooseneck hoes and mule-drawn plows were the only tools available to fight weeds. Thanks to TVA's fertilizer experiment station, fertilizer was available to the farmer which at least made the growing of crops possible.

Ed and Carl kept meticulous records on their cotton crop. It seemed that, no matter how hard they worked to produce a good crop, their effort was lost to insects and weeds. They averaged making a bale of cotton to the acre in 1947, which for the time was excellent production, but they still lost money.

One morning at breakfast, their conversation went something like this: "We made as good a crop as we can expect" Ed said. "Yes, we did. The workers and sharecroppers worked hard, and the weather was favorable, but we still lost money. How can we ever hope to be in the black financially if we continue to raise cotton, because we'll not make this good of a crop each year?" Carl replied. Ed said, "The only answer for us is to diversify with different crops and expand our cattle herd." "That's fine, but it will require a large capital outlay with fencing, livestock purchases, etc., not to mention the fact that we have yet to find a viable permanent pasture grass," Carl said. "I'm going to seriously start looking all over the country and find out if a meaningful, permanent pasture grass exists. I've heard about a grass in Kentucky that sounds pretty good, but I don't know much about it yet," Ed added. "Why don't we just admit right now that life is too short to raise cotton," Carl proposed.

That conversation over the breakfast table was a defining moment in the history of the farm. Ed was good to his promise and diligently searched for a permanent pasture grass. His search eventually led him to Pembroke, Kentucky, where he saw a grass called "Kentucky 31 Fescue" growing luxuriously green on a hillside in the dead of Winter. This grass had been discovered on a Mr. Suiter's farm in Menifee County, Kentucky by Dr. E.N. Fergus of the University of Kentucky in 1931: hence, the numerals "31". Subsequent contact with an area farmer resulted in an agreement to send four combines and tractors to Menifee County, Kentucky to help harvest the farmer's 1948 crop.

One morning in June of 1948, a small "caravan" of tractors, combines, and service trucks began their journey from Huntsville to Kentucky. Most of the men were converted black sharecroppers that had never been out of Madison County, much less the State of Alabama. They stayed in Kentucky about two weeks, slept and ate in the fields, and all reported a grand adventure when they returned. They returned with a lot of stories and about 2,000 pounds of Kentucky 31 Fescue seed.

That Fall, the farm planted 80 acres with this seed, which, as far as we know, was the first planting of Kentucky 31 Fescue outside of the state of Kentucky. This "wonder grass," as it was dubbed, was very popular with all the cattlemen who grew the grass. G.W. Jones and Sons' farm subsequently planted and maintained over 6,000 acres of Kentucky 31 Fescue by the 1970s. By the year 2000, the nation had 35 million acres of Kentucky 31 Fescue pasture grass planted east of the Mississippi River.

G.W. Jones and Sons' farm methodically plowed up the cotton fields and planted fescue on four farms in three North Alabama counties. Around 1,500 acres each on the Madison, Jackson, and Marshall County farms were planted along with 1,800 acres of land on Redstone Arsenal. These plantings fostered major changes in the farm operation. A new seed plant to clean and package Certified Kentucky 31 Fescue was built, which operated until the 1990s. Several cattle purchases were made in order to consume the large amount of forage being grown on these fields. The Fescue crop was very efficient in that the farm could graze the land for nine months and cut seed for three months. In all, it took about 35 men to harvest the seed each year, and the cleaning process took about 120 days.

Kentucky 31 Fescue seed was very popular, and the 50 lb. sacks of cleaned seed were shipped to most of the southeastern states. By the 1970s, G.W. Jones and Sons Farm harvested, cleaned, and packaged over one million pounds of Certified Kentucky 31 Fescue seed annually.

Cattle had to be purchased to complete the plan for the farm and its future. Consequently, Ed made a trip to Texas in 1950 to search for some female cattle to satisfy the need for livestock. Up until that time, the farm had relied on locally purchased cattle whose bloodlines were not very consistent. Ed settled on purchasing 400 head of Hereford heifers, and it was an exciting day when we received his telegram with the message that they would be delivered in late June of 1950. Knowing they were coming caused a flurry of work. Fencing had to be secure, water and mineral points erected, extra hay had to be harvested, and the final transportation of the heifers to the farm arranged. Cattle were shipped long distance via rail cars in those days because the trucks were small and the roads were not very good. On arrival day at the Huntsville Train Depot, the farm had engaged six trucks, all single-axle, 20-feet long, to haul the calves from the train station to the farm.

The cattle were unloaded in the big lot around the 1915 vintage horse barn until they settled down, ate, and learned to drink our water, which is quite different from Texas water. The cattle made the trip well and were good quality calves. Each calf had a brand of 6666 burned high on their rib cage. This reflected the ownership of the ranch from which we made the purchase. The Four-Six Ranch was a famous old ranch in Texas which bred Hereford cattle and is still operating today. Supposedly, the ranch was acquired in a poker game with a four-of-a-kind hand of four sixes. In any event, it was a large ranch and bred good cattle at the time. These Four-Six heifers formed the base of our cattle herd which remained pure Hereford, until we started crossbreeding in the 1980s.

The metamorphosis of changing cotton farmers into cattlemen was difficult at best. One of the main problems was that the sharecroppers were used to giving loud voice commands to their mules. This won't work well with cattle as quieter is better. Some of the sharecroppers refused to make the change from cotton to grass and cattle. One of our favorites, farm philosopher Will Bill Battle, refused to make the change and decided to continue to sharecrop for another farmer. Most stayed, however, and made the conversion and became excellent Alabama cowboys.

In spite of all the work that accompanied the farm with its seed and cattle business, there was always something amusing happening among the workers. One incident involved my father and one of our more colorful characters, a worker named Roy Lee Ford. Roy Lee was a bad apple in any group of workers to which he was assigned. Roy Lee was always bragging about how he was going to "whoop" someone, and was always in a fuss or fight. One night about 2:00 a.m., we got a knock on the door and my father and I reached the front door about the same time. There stood Otha Lee, John K. Eversons's son, with a concerned look on his face. He said, "John K. said to call the police because he done kilt Roy Lee." My father said, "Are you sure he killed him?" "Yesser, he done shot him in the head." With this, we called the police, got dressed, and went up the road to John K.'s house. The police arrived shortly in two police cars, along with an ambulance with flashing lights. One of the officers asked John to describe what happened. John K. said, "I was asleep in the bed, and this smart-ass boy came in and grabbed me and put a cold knife to my neck and told me he was going to kill me." "What did you do?" inquired the officer. John K. didn't hesitate, "I pushed him off'en me and retch up on the mantle and got my pistol and shot him." "Did you mean to kill him?" questioned the officer. "Yes, sir, I sho did," was John's answer.

     The questioning went on between the officer and John K.: "Where was the victim when you shot him?" "On the floor" he replied. "Where were you when you were doing the shooting?" the officer asked. "About two feet right above his head" John K. said. "How many times did you shoot him?" "I think there was nine shells in dar" he answered. "You know I'll have to take you in to the jail overnight because of your intent to kill this man," the officer replied. "Yes, sir," was John K.'s answer.

     At this point, my father spoke up and said to the officer, "Now wait a minute. John is a good man. He has never been in any trouble. And besides, he was in his own house and bed when this man threatened him." "I know, Mr. Carl," the officer said, "but there's been a murder with intent to kill, and I'll have to take him to the jail." About that time, one of the other officers yelled to the ambulance personnel that the victim was not dead and should be taken to the hospital immediately. With that, the ambulance loaded Roy Lee up and, with sirens wailing, rushed to the hospital.

The arresting officer returned to where John, my father, and I were standing and said that, even though the man was not dead, he would still have to take John to jail. John had confessed his intent to kill Roy Lee, so the officer continued to write out his report. "What was the name of the victim?" he inquired of John. "Roy Lee Ford," came the answer. "Roy…. Lee…. Ford. You mean that man in the ambulance was Roy Lee Ford?" the officer exclaimed with disdain. "Yes, sir" he replied. The arresting officer talked with the other officers telling them that the victim was the infamous town troublemaker, Roy Lee Ford. The officer then wadded up the report and threw it on the ground muttering, "I hope he dies."

That was the last John K. heard from the law about the incident. Roy Lee was back at work the next day with nine Band-Aid's on his forehead. John K.'s only comment to the men at the barn was that he would never again load that 22 cal. pistol with "shorts," because in the future he would use the more powerful "long rifle shells and finish the job."

Needless to say, we had very few dull moments on the farm. As a young man, I couldn't have enjoyed life more. Plenty of work, play, adventure, and an array of interesting characters made my boyhood life a real blessing.

There were dozens of funny and interesting incidents like this one during the transition from cotton farming to the cattle business. The rebuilding of the farm was ongoing, and the farm enterprise that Carl and Ed started in 1939 was taking shape.

Cotton, as a main crop, was eventually replaced by a new pasture grass called Kentucky 31 Fescue.

Hereford Cattle Grazing In Jones Valley 1950

Chapter 21 – Huntsville's #1 Salesman

The early 1950s found Huntsville enjoying a significant financial lift from Redstone Arsenal and its activities. Huntsville was experiencing unprecedented growth. By the late 50s, it was not uncommon to see 30 to 50 new subdivisions presented to Huntsville's Planning Commission each month. People from all over the U.S. were finding their way to Huntsville for employment, and a chance to participate in the rocket business.

Huntsville, during this period of rapid growth and influx of people, was still a conservative town that was said by some to have more churches per capita than any city in the United States. The Courthouse Square remained the gathering place for Huntsville's citizens, especially on Saturdays. Most of the socializing and visiting occurred around weekend visits to "the Square."

Carl had been instrumental in forming the Huntsville Industrial Expansion Committee to help cushion Huntsville with industry, in the event that the Arsenal rocket effort ceased or was directed elsewhere. He would serve as chairman of this committee for three terms and had a hand in most of the committee decisions for over fifteen years. One thing the HIEC and Chamber did was to encourage all of Huntsville's citizens to use their influence to promote good will for the Arsenal and its rocket team. There was always the threat that the government would move the rocket team to another location, which would be disastrous for Huntsville. One of the pleas to the community was to make life as pleasant as possible for the military personnel stationed at Redstone.

Thankfully, the arsenal remained intact and even today is still expanding. Redstone Arsenal is, and has been, one of the primary economic drivers of not just Huntsville, but the entire State of Alabama for the last 60 odd years.

During the decade of the 50s, Carl was working tirelessly for the community, as well as balancing time between his family, the farm, and the engineering business. He was on the board of directors of The First National Bank, and was a Rotarian serving as president from 1949-50. He served seven years on the Board of the Huntsville Madison County Chamber of Commerce. Carl was a leader behind much of the industrial expansion in Madison County. Industries such as the Norton Company, Wyle Laboratories, Mallory Capacitor Company, Linde Company, Automatic Electric, Dunlop Tire and Rubber Company, Barber Coleman, and the Pittsburgh Plate Glass (PPG) Company, to name a few, relocated to Huntsville during this time period. These businesses, and many others, came partly due to the personal touch of the hand of Carl Jones. Someone thoughtfully nicknamed him "Huntsville's #1 Salesman" during this era.

In order to be a good salesman, the salesman has to totally believe in his product. This was true with Carl Jones; he loved and believed in Huntsville and North Alabama . He became a much sought-after speaker, and most of these speeches extolled the virtues of North Alabama. His talks usually described Alabama as a state rich in natural resources, water, and an ideal climate. Alabama's most valuable resource, he maintained, was its people.

An honest, hardworking, conservative workforce that would make any company interested in relocating to the Huntsville area.

Carl had a saying that I still hear sometimes even today: "Those people who were born in Madison County were just plain lucky, and those who moved here were just plain smart." His love for the area spilled over into everything he did.

One of Carl's major accomplishments for the community was to form a group of businessmen to purchase a sliver of land on the northern edge of Redstone Arsenal. This sliver of land had been severed from the arsenal by the new Alabama Highway 20 and served no future use for the military installation. Pooling their money, this land was purchased under the name of the Huntsville Industrial Sites (HIS) with Carl Jones as its president. Several industries bought land from HIS, and some remain there today. In the process, the HIS group made a substantial profit. Rather than simply distribute the money to its members, the HIS group, at Carl's urging, chose to contribute its profit to The University of Alabama in Huntsville. There was no foundation to receive these funds at UAH at that time, so they formed one. The UAH Foundation is still in existence today, and has been very influential and supportive of UAH over the years.

Throughout the years, Huntsville's citizens have continued to contribute land, money, and other valuables to UAH through this Foundation. Dr. Wernher von Braun also influenced significant support of UAH by telling Carl and Huntsville's leadership that, "It is impossible to have a 'high tech' community without a meaningful research institute such as UAH." UAH has played a major role in Huntsville's becoming a "high tech" community, a role that was originally fostered and supported by the Huntsville Industrial Sites group.

During this growth period of the 1950s, Carl continued to juggle his many activities in the community with the family, farm, and engineering business. Always expanding, Carl teamed up with a longtime friend from Birmingham, Dr. Milton Fies, to purchase 44,000 acres of mineral rights in Jackson County. Dr. Fies was a metallurgist and had spent most of his life developing underground mines near Birmingham. Dr. Fies was convinced that this tract of land near the town of Flatrock would prove to be a profitable surface mining venture. Subsequently, the Carl Jones Family and the Milton Fies Family formed the North Alabama Mineral Development Company.

The coal seams on the property are thin, but the BTU level is good with a low sulfur content, which makes it marketable. Coal production from these lands has mostly been steam coal, which was sold to the nearby TVA Widow's Creek Steam Plant. This successful venture again showed that Carl was a forward thinker and he became a partner with many other visionaries in Alabama.

Through the late 40s and into the 50s, Carl made many close friends who eventually became involved in several of these ventures. In college, Carl lived with two friends, James E. Davis and J.D. Hays, in Garland Hall at the University of Alabama. These three remained lifelong friends. James and J.D. both went by the name "Jimmy," and both Jimmys and their families were entwined with our family. Other friends and associates that were very close to the Carl Jones Family were Louis Salmon, our attorney, David Johnston, our CPA, and Beirne Spragins, our banker, to name a few. These, along with a cadre of other friends and business associates formed a close, effective network that served the community well.

Several industrial and research parks were envisioned by these men and others which have resulted in some of today's success of the Huntsville area. The original Research Park, Thornton Research Park, Lowe Industrial Park, Chase Industrial Park, and several smaller tracts were birthed by these men in the 1950s and early 60s. Carl's engineering expertise and his engineering firm, G.W. Jones and Sons, was invaluable in putting these parks together. In many cases, the land was donated to the UAH Foundation, which subsequently developed the tract by designing and overseeing roads and other infrastructure necessary to suit a prospective industry. The City of Huntsville mostly constructed these roads and infrastructure. The idea was to have a vacant tract of land ready for an industrial or research-oriented prospect when they came calling. The process worked well, and when the Foundation made a profit, it was passed on to UAH in the form of scholarships and other support.

John E. Hatch, former chamber president, once wrote in a letter that Carl Jones was the dynamo behind marketing these tracts. Hatch went on to say that, if a prospect was too tough, someone would always say, "Let Carl have him." I still have that letter today and treasure it. All of these men were part of "The

Greatest Generation" that led our county after World War II. For Huntsville and Madison County during this time frame, there was no doubt that Carl Jones was Huntsville's #1 Salesman.

Thornton Research Park

Chapter 22 – Mister Carl

In the late 50s, Ed and Carl decided to expand their farming operation. Somehow they felt that farming would someday eclipse anything else they attempted. To this end, they wanted to expand their pasture acreage, so they leased 1,800 acres from Redstone Arsenal and decided to purchase a 4,500 acre farm in Jackson County. All of these lands had the same production goal of raising fescue seed and cattle.

By the late 50s, the fescue grass was growing well, producing good grazing and seed. The cattle, however, were not growing well and ran an elevated body temperature in the months of May and October. At first this malady was blamed on genetics, then on parasites, neither of which was correct. It would be three decades before a discovery surfaced proving that the root cause of the poor beef production was an unseen fungus within the grass. Unaware of this information, Ed and Carl sought to further diversify the livestock end of the business. They purchased bulls from several different bloodlines, changed their mineral mix, and paid veterinarians and research people a lot of money to diagnose the problem. They even decided to go into the sheep business, desperately searching for an answer to make their fescue pasture more productive.

A lot of effort had been expended on the farm, so Ed and Carl asked me to seek an agricultural degree as a way to preserve the farm for the future. This really suited me since I loved growing things and being outside. This was no small decision on their part, because this meant that I would attend the Alabama Polytechnic Institute (Auburn University). All of the family was and had been staunch University of Alabama students and fans. I think I was the most pleased one of the family. Auburn provided a good education for me, and eventually the school provided the answer to our decade-old problem with our fescue and the fever it caused in our cattle.

The sheep venture didn't work out primarily because the South is too soft in its terrain for sheep. Sheep thrive on dry, rocky areas where the abrasive surface wears down their hooves. The hoof of a sheep grows about an inch a week. Left alone, this excess hoof growth will fold under and get infected. We had to trim, by hand, each sheep's feet regularly. Ed and Carl purchased 500 ewes to start the sheep herd. These 500 ewes brought 2,000 feet with them that had to be regularly trimmed. I came home from Auburn one June, and when I went back in September all I had done was trim sheep's feet. I was elated when they decided to get out of the sheep business the following year.

During the 1950s, there were a lot of things that happened to Carl Jones and his family. I went off to Auburn, and my sisters, Betsy and Carolyn, were growing up. Betsy and I were prewar children, born in 1935 and 1939, and Carolyn was a postwar child born in 1948. Also, in addition to all of his businesses and community endeavors, Carl decided to expand his farmhouse in Jones Valley to accommodate his growing family. Originally built in 1823, repairs and remodeling were badly needed.

On top of all these events, Carl lost his partner and brother in 1956. The load of the farm and the engineering business that Ed had been carrying all fell on Carl. Carl would later say that the latter part of the 1950s was the most difficult time of his life. Settling Ed's estate and following through with several heavy business decisions increased Carl's load. The Jackson County farm purchase was pending. Huntsville was growing, and the demand for engineering services was also expanding. Nonetheless, Carl plowed ahead, and with hard work and perseverance he rose to the task of helping the community, family, and business succeed.

All of these events were occurring while Huntsville was growing exponentially. People were flocking to the Huntsville area from all over the country. Many of them had predisposed opinions about this backward state called Alabama and this one-horse town named Huntsville. Yankees were usually the most opinionated and were often unkind in their remarks. I remember one particular story along that line that circulated around the courthouse square during this growth period.

The story happened at the Central Cafe in downtown Huntsville one morning as one of the newly arrived Yankees came in to order breakfast. "What will you have this morning, sir?" asked the waiter. "What do you have on the menu that's good?" the customer asked. "It's all good" he replied. "I would expect you to say that, dummy," the Yankee replied. "I simply want to know what is the best, your specialty, if that's not too difficult for you." "Well," the waiter replied, "We have some mighty good beef tongue." "Beef tongue! You mean the kind that comes out of an animal's mouth?" the Yankee customer replied. "Yes, sir, that's the kind," said the waiter. Very indignant, the customer declared, "I'll have you know that I don't eat anything that comes out of an animal's mouth." "Okay then, what will you have?" said the waiter. "I guess I'll just have a couple of eggs," responded the learned Yankee. The entire restaurant was listening in to this dialog and the place exploded with laughter at the Yankee's last comment. I'm not sure the learned Yankee ever "got it."

Still another duty that Carl took on was serving as Huntsville's City Engineer. Carl accepted this assignment and dealt with a myriad of engineering problems for the politicians and citizenry.

I remember being with him at the office late one afternoon when he received a frantic call that the water tank on Pulaski Pike was in danger of being sucked into a growing sinkhole. We quickly made our way in a pouring down rain to the tank on Pulaski Pike. Utility personnel and others present were greatly concerned about the fate of the tank. A 30x30 foot sinkhole was about 20 feet from the tank and growing. Carl immediately took charge and barked out orders in military fashion to the assembled workers. "Go get six dump trucks and load them with rip rap size stone. Dump and spread those loads in the sinkhole, and then bring six more loads of stone one-half that size," Carl commanded. Carl's voice left no doubt as to what he wanted. Immediately, the idle crews went into action with men scurrying in every direction. Within two hours the sinkhole was plugged and hadn't presented any more problems 60 years later. The sinkhole was a simple "lime sink" that is common throughout the Tennessee Valley. Carl was quick to recognize the problem and took the necessary action to stop the spread of the sinkhole and possibly save the water tank.

On another occasion, Carl received a call from the Allied Mills Company in Guntersville, Alabama. This company owned several soybean silos near the bank of Guntersville Lake. The silos were full of soybeans, about one million bushels, and one was gradually leaning toward the lake. This falling silo and its contents represented a several million dollar loss if it pitched into the lake. Carl called his geologist brother, Walter, and the two of them made several trips to the site. They surmised that this was another lime sink causing the silo's foundation to fail. They were given authority by Allied to expend whatever it took in effort and funds to stop the silo from falling into the lake. Immediately, they engaged a directional drilling company to drill diagonal holes under the silo. They then pumped over 100,000 bags of cement into those drilled holes. This pressurized cement not only stopped the leaning of the silo, but caused it to return toward its original position. Allied asked them to stop raising the silo because it was affecting the alignment of their unloading augers. Allied was most appreciative and extended many compliments on Carl and the G.W. Jones and Sons staff for saving their silo from the lake.

The preceding accomplishments are only a couple of feats performed by Carl Jones and his company during the 1950s. There are dozens more that could be mentioned. Carl was leading his family, company, and community in a wonderful way. Times were good. Huntsville was growing. The farms were expanding, despite the poor cattle production, and Carl was becoming known far and wide as the man leading the way.

Somewhere about this time Carl was tagged with the title of "Mr. Huntsville." I suppose this title was appropriate because he was helpful in leading the charge for the community. He seemed to have boundless energy and had a way of command that compelled people to follow his lead. Whether it was a farm group or a rocket scientist group, there was a yen to follow his suggestions. His demeanor was very compelling.

I once had one of his employees tell me that he would rather be "chewed out" by Carl Jones than complimented by anyone else. Carl had that magic touch, and everyone that came in contact with that touch benefited in some way. Even his antagonists and contemporaries referred to him respectfully as "Mr. Carl."

This was a golden time for the Jones Family and Huntsville. Little did any of them realize but an event by another country on October 4, 1957 would have an even greater impact on North Alabama and particularly Huntsville in the coming decade. Economically, the best was yet to come.

Sheep grazing in Jones Valley, circa 1954

Carl T. Jones, "Mr. Huntsville", circa 1960

Chapter 23 - The HIC Center

On October 4, 1957, Russia launched the world's first orbiting satellite named Sputnik. This event sent shock waves through our government, as well as the American public. Less than a month later, on November 3rd, the Soviets sent up another orbiter with a dog as its passenger. These back-to-back, successful space launches put fear in our population that our cold war enemy was far ahead in technology.

This wake-up call initiated a response from our government. On December 6, 1957, a U.S.A. Navy rocket (Vanguard) carrying a grapefruit-sized satellite rose heavenward only four feet and collapsed in flames. Five days after the Vanguard failure, President Eisenhower gave the green light to the United States Army to launch into orbit a U.S. satellite.

In Huntsville, Alabama, the Redstone team of Dr. Wernher von Braun had been busy for months testing and re-testing the Army's Redstone Intermediate Range Ballistic Missile. One of the leaders of von Braun's team was Major General John B. Medaris. Medaris was a decisive leader and was in charge of operations and implementation of this missile, the Redstone. Medaris promised to have a satellite in orbit within 90 days.

The satellite to be orbited was built by the Jet Propulsion Laboratory of Pasadena, California. The rocket used to propel this satellite (which was named Explorer 1) into orbit was the Jupiter-C. The Jupiter-C was a three-stage missile, and the first stage (and primary lifter) was the Redstone. The rocket blasted off from Cape

Canaveral at 10:48 p.m., January 31, 1958, and successfully orbited as America's first satellite.

Medaris missed his promise of having Explorer 1 in orbit in 90 days. The actual time from his promise to orbit was only 51 days. On that frigid Friday night of January 31st, a rather large crowd which included Carl Jones, assembled around the Madison County Courthouse Square. The reason for the assembly was to listen for a beep over the loudspeaker from Explorer 1, which would confirm the fact that the satellite had successfully orbited the earth. When the signal finally came one hour and forty-five minutes after the launch, the crowd erupted in cheers.

These events evolved into the "Moon Race" between our country and Russia. This race had a profound effect on our nation and especially Huntsville. Competition always seems to bring out the best from the competitors involved. Such was the case of the world's first moon race. America put its best minds and resources into this race. Many things we enjoy today came as a result of it. Computers, solid state transistors, new metal alloys, long-range communication, many satellite uses and space travel to name just a few. Many of these were conceived, designed, and built in the once sleepy little cotton town called Huntsville, Alabama.

Huntsville's population in 1960 was 72,365. The moon race was already swelling the town's borders. Carl had been instrumental in fostering several land expansions of Huntsville's city limits. The real jolt, however, was the influx of people that came in 1962.

The Boeing Company won a large contract for missile technology and production in the early 60s as a result of the moon race. Boeing was, at that time, based primarily in Seattle, Washington. A nationwide search was conducted by Boeing for office space and facilities to work on their new contract. Early in the search, Boeing decided that the ideal place for their efforts would be Huntsville. The problem was that there were no buildings or closely located groups of buildings to house the 6,000 aerospace workers Boeing needed to relocate.

Lincoln Mills was a large textile manufacturing plant in Huntsville that had closed in 1957. The Lincoln Mills facility had enough square footage, but was in rough condition for the aerospace business. Carl and a group of Huntsville businessmen met with Boeing about renovating and using these old mill buildings. The Boeing officials were cool to the idea of Lincoln, but accepted the fact that the size and layout of the buildings would work. Their main objection was that they had to have space that would be operational in 90 days.

Carl convinced the Boeing group that if they would agree to lease the old mill, that Huntsville would have it ready within 60 days of the agreement. Boeing thought this was an impossible task, but with no other Huntsville alternative, they signed on to the agreement.

Carl and some of his business associates formed a corporation named the Huntsville Industrial Associates (HIA) and purchased Lincoln Mills. At a frantic pace they hired every contractor available in the area to work on the renovations. The old building buzzed with workers, guided by architects and engineers, until it was completed in 59 days, with one day to spare.

The impact of 6,000 immediate aerospace jobs caused some real growing pains within the city. Most of the workers came to Huntsville kicking and screaming. They didn't want to leave Seattle and come to this backwoods state called Alabama, much less to work in an old cotton mill building. To appease these complaints, Boeing gave them the option of moving to the Michoud Ordnance Plant in Louisiana after one year in Huntsville. Michoud was Boeing's second choice for their relocation since they already had existing facilities there.

The Chamber of Commerce kept up with the requests for transfer to Michoud. Approximately 70% of the Boeing transfers made a formal request to be relocated to Michoud in Louisiana. By the time the required year was over, about half of those had chosen to stay in Huntsville, Alabama. Within another year, about 90% of those that had moved to South Louisiana had returned to Huntsville. This proved to be quite a compliment to the southern hospitality and warmth of John Hunt's old town.

These 6,000 jobs, with their $30 million annual payroll, was a major catalyst in propelling Huntsville into being dubbed as the "Space Capital of the World." New businesses, buildings, subdivisions and churches sprang up rapidly during this space race period of the early 60s. The HIA venture became very profitable and would subsequently add to its presence and influence on the city. HIA used its rental cash from the HIC facility (the name attached to the old mill, which was an acronym for the Huntsville

Industrial Center) to purchase the State National Bank building downtown. Some years later, the group would build the Huntsville Hilton Hotel and purchase the Research Park buildings of Astro Space and BellSouth. In addition to these, the HIA contributed to many charitable and other business endeavors in the state, city, and county.

The HIA group eventually became the first Real Estate Investment Trust in the state of Alabama. Another fortunate aspect of the HIC venture for Huntsville was that these businessmen of HIA plowed their money back into the community. Men like Louis Salmon, David Johnston, Charles Eifler, Jimmy Davis, Jimmy Hays, Tom Thrasher, and others skillfully guided this very successful venture, a venture that would last into the next century.

The statesman, Sir Winston Churchill, called the years during the World War II German blitz of England, "Britain's finest hour." The early 60s, the space race, and handling the growth of Huntsville very well may have been "Huntsville's finest hour." The city limits expanded from four square miles to 100 square miles. The City added a schoolroom a week to accommodate the influx of young families. It was said that Huntsville had more churches per capita than any city in the nation, and was a conservative, relatively crime-free town that received accolades from all over the nation. Voted as the best place to live in the nation on several occasions, and nicknamed the "Rocket City," this sleepy little cotton town had made a name for itself.

It was during the early 1960s that the Chamber of Commerce initiated a slogan contest. The winning slogan of 25 words or less that complimented Huntsville would receive a prize of $25. The winning slogan was "Huntsville has what it takes to make a good home for me and my family." The winner was Betty Jones, wife of Carl Jones. Winning the contest thrilled my mother and her slogan truly reflected the spirit of Huntsville at the time.

HSV Times newspaper announcing Explorer I satellite

Gathering at Court House Square, Jan 31, 1958

Chapter 24 - Exciting Times

The growth and expansion of Huntsville during the early 60s seemed to be a team effort. There was a "unity of spirit and a bond of peace" among our citizens and government officials. It seemed that the people of Huntsville and Madison County worked for one purpose - to encourage, foster, and manage the rapid growth that was occurring. Unlike today, there were very few factions and regulations that stymied growth. This could have been because of the town's relief from the war and not having to depend solely on agriculture or cotton mills. Whatever the reason, Huntsville's population reflected the same will of the people to work that is recorded in Nehemiah 4:6, which reads: *"So built we the wall;…for the people had a mind to work."*

The Carl Jones Family also exhibited this same will to work during this time. I received my B.S. Degree in Agriculture from Auburn University in 1957. That same year, I was commissioned a 2nd lieutenant in the National Guard. Upon completing my military training obligations, I returned home to manage the farms. On September 4, 1960, I married Elizabeth Ann Mercer, a schoolteacher, and moved into one of the houses on the farm.

Betsy, my sister, married Peter L. Lowe in 1961, and Peter started working at the office doing appraisal and other real estate-related work. My youngest sister, Carolyn, was still at home and attending school.

The farm continued to expand with land purchases in Jackson and Marshall Counties. The operational goals of the farms were still cattle and seed production. The seed production methods remained fairly constant from a management standpoint. The cattle herd, however, needed improvement and, consequently, I was dispatched to Texas to search for a seed stock source that would improve the herd's genetics. Several trips to Texas were made, and quite a number of bulls and heifers were brought back to the farm. The cattle herd consisted of about 1,200 females at the time, which were all of the Hereford breed. Annual farm sales in the early 60s totaled about 1,000 calves and about 800,000 lbs. of Certified Kentucky 31 Fescue Seed.

Somehow, Carl oversaw the entire operation of G.W. Jones and Sons. He kept up with the activities on the farm, as well as the engineering business. Carl was at the office by 8 a.m. each day to deal with a bevy of engineering problems and projects. Interspersed in his day, and many times into the night, were his community obligations. City council meetings, HIEC duties, HIA, and HIC problems were all a drain on his time and energy. Even with all of his duties, Carl seemed to thrive on hard work.

Despite all of his obligations, Carl found time to hunt with me and travel with my mother. A small farm near Swancott, Alabama, in southeast Limestone County became a favorite duck hunting place. Some of Carl's most enjoyable hunts were with his brother, Walter, his friend Jimmy Hays, and me. Ducks and geese were in abundance at that time, and these waterfowl hunts occurred whenever the opportunity presented itself. Carl also used this hunting place to entertain visiting industrial leaders that came looking for possible relocation to the Huntsville area.

One of the more interesting projects G.W. Jones & Sons and Carl were called on to perform during the early 60s was the mapping of a cave under the Madison County Courthouse. The courthouse is located on a rather high bluff overlooking the Big Spring in downtown Huntsville. There is a narrow cave in this bluff through which a large spring flows to the west. This is the Big Spring where Isaac Criner camped in 1804 on his initial trip to North Alabama. The millions of gallons of water that flowed from the spring had, over time, formed this narrow cave in the rock bluff.

The reason for the survey was to correctly locate the cave. A new courthouse was being designed, and the weight of the new structure needed to rest on an area which would not be impacted by the cave. Today, as one observes the courthouse, it will be noticed that the weight of the building is on the south side of the lot. The north side of the courthouse lot is where the cave is located. From the spring outlet, the cave meanders east dissecting the courthouse lot.

Carl called on Walter, his brother, to head up this caving expedition. Being an excellent caver, and geologist, Walter organized the men and the task. I was involved along with four volunteers from the survey crews. Peter Lowe also went underground for several days and kept notes.

The entrance to the cave was from a ledge just north of the old First National Bank building. There was a drop of about 20 feet to the stream flowing through the cave. We used a rope ladder to descend into the flowing stream. I was the first one down the ladder and dropped about three feet into the waist-high cold spring water.

The flow of the stream had been diminished somewhat by the fact that it was a dry August, and the city water pumps were purposely being pumped to capacity to reduce the flow for the survey effort. Even with these reduced water flow conditions, we found it necessary to construct "catwalks" from this drop point to a big room not far from the entrance. This big room lies directly under Jefferson Street just west of the courthouse.

The caving survey took about three weeks. The mapping crew would go in early in the morning, map all day, and come out at dusk. At noon, someone would bring lunch down the ladder, and we would eat in the big room. By using a measuring tape and a small transit to turn angles, we finally located a point for a drill hole in the big room. After this hole was complete, we dropped an electrical wire into the cave and thereafter, we ate and did some of our work by light, which was helpful in the pitch black darkness of the cave.

The finished cave map showed cross-sections every 50 feet, which included the width, height, and floor consistency of the cave. We mapped the cave, which was really a water fissure, from the Big Spring in an easterly direction all the way under the courthouse lot. From that point, we continued east into and through the next block and exited the cave through a manhole in front of the old YMCA building.

Cave Picture: Walter Jones holding a map / Ray Jones holding the rope ladder

Each day, the muddy crew emerged with tales of the cave. Evidence of people before us in the cave was found each day. Evidently, in the 1920s, there was an effort to wall off the cave and its water. The apparent thinking was that a yellow fever outbreak came from the town's Big Spring water supply. The real source of the yellow fever outbreak was later assigned to the mosquito and its bite.

The cave mapping project was the talk of the town, and the caving crew was in the news regularly. This project was just one of many interesting tasks for Carl and G.W. Jones & Sons in the early 1960s.

Another engineering task for Carl and G.W. Jones and Sons was to try and keep Huntsville's old airport operational. Huntsville had a small airport in the early 60s that boasted three airline carriers: Capital Airlines, Southern Airways, and Eastern Airlines. The airport was reportedly named "You Bet Your Life" by the airline pilots. Just off the southern end of the runway was a rock quarry. This quarry and the surrounding topography required a steep approach of any aircraft when landing into a north wind, hence the name. Even though it looked dangerous, the safety record showed no accidents ever occurred. The airport was vacated in 1967.

Even though Huntsville's air travel numbers were small, the growing size of the arsenal and the increased space effort demanded regular flights, mostly to Washington D.C. The general public was also beginning to use the airlines on a regular basis. One story that occurred about this time involved a flight to Huntsville from Atlanta. It seems that a somewhat uninformed man went to the Capital Airline ticket counter and asked about buying a ticket to Huntsville. "Yes, sir," the agent said, "that will cost you $42.60." "That's fine," said the customer, "what time does it take off?" "Takeoff is at 9:20 a.m., and it arrives in Huntsville at 8:10 a.m.," the agent responded. Not realizing the change in time zones, the customer asked the agent to repeat the takeoff and arrival times. The agent complied and asked if the man wanted a ticket. "No, sir, I don't believe I do," the customer replied. He continued after repeating the time by saying, "But if you don't mind, I'd like to hang around and watch that thing take off."

Huntsville badly needed a meaningful airport, and its leadership was searching for a way to build one. The mid 1960s would see that dream come true with a larger international airport far away from the rock quarry.

Old Airport Terminal

Chapter 25 - The New Airport

One of Carl's best friends, Ed Mitchell, hurriedly made his way into Carl's office one Monday morning. "Carl, cancel whatever you're doing and come with me for a few minutes," he said. Carl complied, and they rode to the western side of the county. Ed stopped the car and asked Carl to look south from Alabama Highway 20. Ed said that the Huntsville Madison County Airport Authority (HMCAA) had received preliminary approval from the FAA to purchase about 3,000 acres along County Line Road for a new airport. Ed was like a little kid with a new toy and could hardly contain his enthusiasm.

In the coming months, Ed's vision began to take root and became a reality. Farms were purchased in that area and the preliminary design for an airport began to take shape. Early on, a major problem surfaced in that this chosen site was not in the city of Huntsville. Huntsville had to be involved, since most of the routine services to support a large airport had to be rendered by a city.

Carl came to the rescue by identifying a one-mile wide corridor from the Huntsville city limits to the new airport site. The only problem was that most of this corridor was on Redstone Arsenal land. After many trips to Washington, Carl and the local authorities convinced the Pentagon to allow the corridor lands to be annexed into the City of Huntsville. Other problems, of course, would surface until the airport opened in the Fall of 1967, but the corridor issue was a major one.

Ed and the HMCAA called on G.W. Jones & Sons to be their design engineering firm for the new airport. The airport would have parallel runways one mile apart that would eventually reach 12,600 and 10,000 feet in length. An intermodal air cargo center (later named the J.E. "Ed" Mitchell International Intermodal Center) was envisioned that would accommodate international flights daily. Passenger numbers would reach a peak by 2005 at 1,265,671. The airport still boasts one of the largest import/export centers in the nation based on acreage. No doubt the emergence of this airport has been very valuable to progress of the city, state, and nation.

Dr. Walter B. Jones was called on to solve a problem that occurred during the runway construction. The west runway was well underway when a small cave was uncovered in the center of the runway. Work was stopped while Walter put on his caving attire and researched the cave. After several hours underground, Walter determined that the cave was small, about 50 yards in diameter with a 12-foot ceiling. Walter correctly deducted that the cave was self-contained, and that there was no danger of the cave leaking or causing settlement which would damage the runway above.

Walter then ordered several cases of dynamite and strategically placed the explosives at points designed to collapse the cave in place. This took several hours, but it took only seconds to collapse the cave. Today, various regulations would probably hold up construction for weeks on such an incident. After the explosion, construction continued the following day. That was in 1967, and to date the runway has never had a base failure.

The airport has grown into a regional hub and an economic driver for the Tennessee Valley. Over the years, the airport and its engineering design has received numerous awards and recognitions. This airport complex that was designed by Carl and G.W. Jones & Sons, received a National Achievement Award from the American Consulting Engineers Council in 1968.

The airport and its success vaulted Carl and G.W. Jones & Sons Consulting Engineers into being very sought after in the engineering world. Calls and requests from municipalities and customers came in increasing numbers. Somehow, Carl was able to deal with these engineering requests and projects. Still, he remained active with the farm and its operation. The community leaders seemed to call on him more each day to address the problems of Huntsville's growing community. As stated in an earlier chapter, Carl was called on to outline and sell several city annex expansions. Carl and his firm designed and implemented Huntsville's sewage treatment plant disposal system, as well as numerous roads and subdivisions. Huntsville was growing, and Carl, along with the engineering firm, and his cadre of business associates were leading that growth.

At one of Carl's many meetings, he became convinced that the moon race would be successfully won by our country. The downside to winning the moon race would be that Huntsville would have to sustain itself economically from other sources, once we visited the moon. The group of businessmen in that meeting felt that there would be nothing of value on the moon. The adventure and quest to get there was a real economic value to our city. But what then?

The group was convinced that the city should not wait for the inevitable, but should actively seek an alternative source of employment and income for Huntsville. The Madison County Commission subsequently authorized Carl to obligate land, site work, and utility services that might be necessary to entice industries to locate in Madison County. They had confidence in Carl, knowing that he would do what was fair and not abuse the municipality involved. Carl moved out on his new assignment with his usual vigor and enthusiasm.

After many out-of-town trips in pursuit of new industries, Carl and the community leadership focused on four prospects: Automatic Electric Company (2,800 jobs), Barber Coleman Co. (400 jobs), PPG (500 jobs), and Dunlop Tire & Rubber Co. (800 jobs). These were all non-union (at that time, Dunlop was non-union, but later become a union company which in large part, in my opinion, is why they are not here today) clean industries that would go a long way toward filling the economic hole that most likely would be left after the end of the moon race.

Carl and the community leadership were able to convince these industries to locate plants within Madison County by 1967. Almost 5,000 jobs came with these industries, which was very helpful to our local economy. The group was right in that there were no real resources to be mined from the moon, not even "green cheese."

Even though Carl never sought the limelight, and many of his civic contributions were never publicized, the citizens of Huntsville knew what his vision and years of dedicated service meant to the community. In 1965, the Huntsville Madison County Chamber of Commerce presented him with its "Distinguished Citizen Award." Carl was at the pinnacle of his success and drew his family, firm, and friends along with him.

In a span of twenty years after returning from fighting in World War II, Carl had become a very successful farmer, businessman, engineer, family man, and community leader. Carl's name had become a household name, familiar to most families in Madison County. Carl had an influence and offered guidance on most major community and business decisions in Madison County during this period of time. Unfortunately, like most things in life, especially the good things, situations are altered and changed by disaster. Such would be the case when this great community leader named Carl T. Jones would suddenly be taken from the scene.

Airport Cave Explosion/1967

Chapter 26 - The Loss

On October 6, 1967, Carl, Walter and I went dove hunting in Limestone County. Carl and Betty had just returned from a trip to Europe with their good friends, Jimmy and Annie Wade Hays. Carl was in excellent spirits, glad to be back home and to be hunting. We had a good hunt, even though Carl said he didn't shoot as well as usual. He blamed the trip and the jet lag he was experiencing. It was a Friday night, and we had planned to go see Huntsville High School play football. Carl called just before I left and said he was tired and passed on going to the game. I don't remember much about the game except that the chainmen got into a fight during the third quarter. The game was stopped until another set of chainmen could be recruited. I stopped by Carl's house on the way home and told him about the chainmen fight, and we had a good laugh.

The next morning, October 7, 1967, he and I met at the barn, and I caught him up on the farm activities. He ate breakfast with Betty and went to the office. Sometime during the morning he went to Johnson & Mahoney, a local men's store, and bought a hat and a new suit. After an early lunch, Carl, Betty, Betsy, and Peter went to see the Alabama/Ole Miss football game in Birmingham. During the second quarter of the game, Carl passed away as a result of a massive heart attack.

At age 58, Carl T. Jones, the great-grandson of Isaac Criner, Madison County's first white settler, was gone. He was at the pinnacle of his career and his family, as well as the community, mourned the loss of this outstanding leader. Expressions of sympathy from people all over the nation reached the family. Grown men openly wept by the side of his casket. Employees, friends, family, and business associates were all stunned at the loss of the man dearly known by most simply as "Mr. Carl."

One indelible impression I shall never forget during this time of mourning was to see a bank president and one of the farm laborers standing together, near his flag-draped casket, weeping for my father. Carl Jones was beloved by the rich and poor, educated and uneducated, and people from all walks of life. The Huntsville Times newspaper had an editorial several weeks following Mr. Carl's death that stated, "The death of Carl Jones still seems to hang heavy over the business community."

Mr. Carl's life was honored in several ways. One was the re-naming of the new Huntsville Madison County Airport, the Carl T. Jones Field. A bronze bust in the airport's main lobby was unveiled at a dedication ceremony some time later. I still see it when I go to the airport and gratefully think of him each time. The family chose to name the four-lane divided highway crossing through the farm, "Carl T. Jones Drive," in honor of their patriarch.

The end of an era had come to a close for the Carl Jones family, as well as the community and all those who knew him. During his lifetime, "Mr. Carl" had served well in so many capacities: as a father, soldier, farmer, businessman, community leader, banker, engineer, and one of Huntsville's most beloved citizens.

G.W. JONES & SONS, CONSULTING ENGINEERS

The engineering firm that was started by G.W. Jones in 1886, continued serving for 127 years until its sale in 2013. Carl and his brother, Ed, grew the firm after the war into a diversified engineering design firm. Hundreds of miles of roads in Huntsville and Madison County were designed by this homegrown engineering firm. The two airports serving the Huntsville area were designed in large part by G.W. Jones & Sons, namely the Huntsville-Madison County International Airport (Carl T. Jones Field) and the Madison County Executive Airport.

In another engineering design category, most of Huntsville's waste water passes through outfall lines designed by G.W. Jones & Sons.

The Harvest-Monrovia Water Treatment plant and appurtenances were also designed by G.W. Jones & Sons. This 10 MGD plant won the State of Alabama's best plant award for three years running. Additionally, thousands of land surveys were performed and many major and secondary roads and bridges were designed over the life of the firm of G.W. Jones & Sons by a wonderful group of employees.

The "office," as it was affectionately called, was composed of a group of workers that worked as a team. Whether the task was a multi-million dollar design project or a lot survey, each task received the same commitment of excellence. The intent, which began in 1886, was to assure each customer that his job was "special" and G.W. Jones himself coined a phrase in 1886 when he went into business:

"A satisfied customer is our first consideration."

Some of the more meaningful recognitions of G.W. Jones & Sons engineering firm over the years are listed below:

1968	State of Alabama's Award for Outstanding Civil Design of Carl T. Jones Field
1987	National Engineering Excellence Award; CTJ Field, Centerline Touchdown Zone Lighting
1987	National Engineering Excellence Award; CTJ Field, Intermodal Center
1987	State of Alabama; Engineering Excellence Award for the International Intermodal Center
2001	State of Alabama; Huntsville Madison County Executive Airport Award
2007	Inducted in the Alabama Engineering Hall of Fame

_____

G.W. JONES & SONS FARMS

The farm that Carl and Ed Jones purchased in 1939 has continued to be a viable entity for over 75 years. Today, the farm in Jones Valley is considered by many to be the largest working urban farm in America. The overall farm enterprise has grown and expanded into four other counties. The headquarters has remained at the original "home place" that Carl and Ed started with in 1939.

Since the "home place" is so visible and accessible to Huntsville's population, it has received the most recognition. Numerous agricultural tours have been hosted over the years. City organizations, college students, and county agricultural groups from Alabama and other states, as well as local kindergarten and grade schools make annual visits to this farm.

We are so grateful for the recognition that the G.W. Jones & Sons Farm has received. We were selected as the "Environmental Stewardship Award" winner for the southeastern United States in 1995. In June of 1996, the farm was named Alabama's "Farm of Distinction" by the Farm-City Committee of Alabama. The Farm-City Committee erected a large sign announcing this award on the Jones Valley Farm for the remainder of 1996.

Also, in 1996, the farm was chosen to represent Alabama in the Lancaster/Sunbelt Expo Southeastern Farmer of the Year recognition in Moutrie, Georgia. This Ag Expo is one of the largest agricultural events in the United States. Competition from farms in eight Southeastern states were represented. We were all elated when G.W. Jones & Sons Farm was chosen as winner of the Expo's farmer of the year award. This event alone caused around 1600 visitors to tour the farm within the following year.

In 2009, the Jackson County farm received the prestigious "Helen B. Mosley Memorial Treasure Forest" award. All three farms have served as host for numerous field days and as a special meeting place for organizations over the years.

The farm in Jones Valley remains very popular with Huntsville's citizens. People like to see the cattle, especially in the Fall when they are calving. I think Ed and Carl would be very pleased that their fledgling 1939 farm enterprise has remained active through the years and has received these accolades.

The Bible says that we reap what we sow in life. Obviously, Carl and Ed Jones sowed some of the right kind of seed. Seeds such as hard work, honesty, integrity, faithfulness, and perseverance must have been in their bag of seed, or the farm would not have lasted this long.

My prayer is that succeeding generations of our family will also garner these same attributes that have flowed down through the years all the way from Madison County's first white settler, Isaac Criner.

As for me personally, I feel most blessed to be blood kin to the patriarchs mentioned in this book. In researching their lives, I was very humbled that they were my ancestors. Their contributions and achievements were significant and meaningful to many people. I chose to close this book with the death of my father, Carl T. Jones, who was not just my father, but my role model, my friend, my business partner, and hunting buddy. I shall forever be grateful that God blessed me to be counted in the lineage of Isaac Criner, G.W. Jones, and especially my beloved father, Carl T. Jones.

Raymond B. Jones

EPILOGUE

I chose to end this book and the story of Isaac Criner's family with the death of my father, Carl T. Jones. The TV commentator, Tom Brokaw, dubbed my father's generation as the "greatest generation." They truly were great and persevered through World War II and the rebuilding of our nation after that war. They were depression kids, and they not only won that worldwide conflict, but launched an economic recovery second to none in our nation's history. Uncharacteristic of victors of other wars in history, America also helped restore and rebuild their enemy's war-torn land, especially in Europe, by rebuilding much of the infrastructure that was devastated by that terrible war. As a nation, our country did what the Bible instructs in Luke 6:31: "And as you would that men should do to you, do you also unto them likewise."

As great as that generation was during the 1940s and the 1950s, I do not think they were the greatest generation. The hardest task assigned to man in this life is that of raising children. Therefore, I believe that the parents of that generation were the greatest. Those parents somehow instilled a sense of ethics and hard work that bore well during those troublesome years. Honesty, integrity, respect, and a drive to never give up permeated their lives. Worthy attributes that we seem to have lost over the last 50 years. Brokaw's "greatest generation" was saturated with principles influenced by the Bible. Even the families who were not religious were influenced by members of their peer group and our elected leaders who exuded Christianity at every level. Almost every politician, soldier, and community leader sought and wanted a Christian influence on that generation of young kids that lived prior to World War II.

School started its day with a Scripture reading, prayer, and the Pledge of Allegiance to the flag. Politicians and others of influence made sure that prayer was said at all public gatherings. Speeches and writings of the day contained Scripture and references to God, patriotism, and country. Brokaw's "greatest generation" was thoroughly influenced by their parents and grew up with a measure of honor and principle that made them truly great. They didn't get it by chance, but by the direction and sincerity of their parents. Parents that, in my view, raised a great generation that saved America and millions of others around the world.

My prayer for the future of our country is that we all strive toward influencing and raising another great generation. In that prayer, we should petition our Heavenly Father to arm us with similar teaching talents that were exhibited by the parents of Brokaw's "greatest generation."

Raymond B. Jones